THE CENTERS OF CIVILIZATION SERIES

ANTIOCH

In the Age of Theodosius the Great

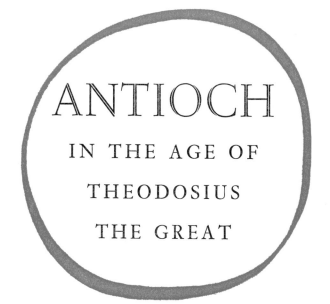

ANTIOCH

IN THE AGE OF

THEODOSIUS

THE GREAT

BY GLANVILLE DOWNEY

NORMAN: UNIVERSITY OF OKLAHOMA PRESS

LIBRARY OF CONGRESS CATALOG CARD NUMBER: 62-16481

COPYRIGHT 1962 BY THE UNIVERSITY OF OKLAHOMA PRESS,
PUBLISHING DIVISION OF THE UNIVERSITY.
COMPOSED AND PRINTED AT NORMAN, OKLAHOMA, U.S.A.,
BY THE UNIVERSITY OF OKLAHOMA PRESS. FIRST EDITION.

To E. Felix Kloman

PREFACE

MAN, in the thought-world of Greece, was in large part the product of the city in which he lived. It was within the city that human civilization was considered to have reached its highest development. Indeed, it was believed that it was primarily in the city, in the context of the good society, that civilization could come to its full flowering, and it is not difficult to understand how Plato and Aristotle were led, by their observation of the culture around them, to devote some of their best thought to the analysis of the ideal city and its society.

In the study of the ancient city, Antioch in Syria has always been a singularly instructive example of the Graeco-Roman city, exhibiting as it does under many aspects the interaction of the varied elements of which the city was made up, and showing the development of the tradition which was shaped by these elements. The present volume endeavors to show what this tradition had come to be in the latter part of the fourth century after Christ, the period of the city's greatest prosperity under the Roman Empire. It is at this period that we have an unusual richness of sources for the history of Antioch, archaeological as well as literary. At this time Antioch, the classical polis, was gradually being transformd into a new kind of city, in which was worked out the new Greek Christian culture which laid the basis for the Byzantine world. This legacy, as handed on to Constantinople, the Byzantine capital, by Antioch and other cities, is portrayed in my book *Constantinople in the Age of Justinian*, written for this series. Thus the heritage of Antioch, preserved and transmitted by Constantinople, has become a part of our own culture.

Two other volumes in The Centers of Civilization Series which will serve as background are *Athens in the Age of Pericles*, by Charles Alexander Robinson, Jr., and *Rome in the Age of Augustus*, by Henry Thompson Rowell.

A significant result of such a study is to underline the ancient regard for the role of the past as an element in the formation of the present and in the preparation of the future. In both pagan and Christian thought—though of course in different terms—the past provided resources for the present and offered some assurance for the stability of the future. As men in classical times learned from the history of their own past, we today may come to a better understanding of our own world by study of its origins.

It was my privilege and good fortune to be allowed to take part in the exploration of Antioch during the first season of the excavations which were conducted from 1932 to 1939. Study of the history of the city, begun then, culminated in the publication of this book and another on Antioch.

In writing any book a scholar reaps where others have labored, and I am aware of my debt to so many others that their names cannot be listed here. For permission to use the quotation in Chapter VI from the late Professor Laistner's translation of John Chrysostom printed in his book *Christianity and Pagan Culture in the Later Roman Empire*, I am indebted to the Cornell University Press. The passage quoted in the same chapter from Canon Telfer's translation of Nemesius of Emesa, *On the Nature of Man,* is quoted by gracious permission of Canon Telfer, the Student Christian Movement Press, Ltd., and the Westminster Press. The passages from Chrysostom's treatise *On the Priesthood* quoted in Chapters VI and VII are based, with grateful acknowledgment, on the version of the Reverend T. P. Brandram printed in *The Select Library of the Nicene and Post-Nicene Fathers of the Christian Church,* First Series, Vol. IX. The quotations of my own translation of Libanius' *Antiochikos* which appear in several chapters are reprinted, with the kind permission of the American Philosophical Society, from the complete translation of the *Antiochikos* published in the *Proceedings* of the Society, Vol. CIII, No. 5 (October, 1959). The quotation from a sermon of Chrysostom printed on page 141 is reproduced from J. H. Srawley's *The Early History of the Liturgy,* second edition, pages 84–85, by permission of the Cambridge University Press.

The restored map of Antioch, drawn at the University of Oklahoma Press especially for this volume, is based on the map in my *History of Antioch in Syria,* published by the Princeton University Press in 1961.

Finally, my thanks go to Professor William M. Calder III of Columbia University, who read the manuscript with a care and interest for which all readers of this book should be grateful. Among the many improvements for which I am indebted to Professor Calder is the metrical version of the inscription quoted in Chapter II, which I had translated only into prose.

G. D.

Dumbarton Oaks,
Washington, D. C.
August, 1962

CONTENTS

Preface   ix
I. "Fair Crown of the Orient"   3
II. A Tour of the City   16
III. The Christian Roman Empire   38
IV. The Good Fortune of Antioch   58
V. The Old World of Libanius   85
VI. John Chrysostom's New World   103
VII. The Holy Mysteries   133
VIII. Old and New: Past and Future   146
Selected Bibliography   157
Index   160

*Map of Antioch, restored as of
the Age of Theodosius the Great*   23

ways a lovely spot, was now much smaller than the large centers which had outgrown it. Gaza, the little university town on the coast of Palestine, was delightful, but like Athens it could not rival the attractions of a large and prosperous provincial capital; and Antioch was not merely a provincial capital but was the headquarters of the Diocese of the Orient, one of the most important political divisions in the eastern half of the empire.

People came, indeed, not only to see the games but to explore the city and admire its magnificent buildings and the spectacular scenery in which it was set. They came, too, to purchase the luxury goods for which the city was famous —fine leather shoes, perfume, spices, textiles, jewelry, books, and the productions of the gold- and silversmiths who had had a first place among the city's craftsmen ever since it had been founded (300 B.C.) by Seleucus the Conqueror 680 years before. A visit to Antioch was one of the best-appreciated pleasures of a world which had always, since the days of Herodotus, held travel to be essential to the formation of a well-informed mind and a cultivated taste. Every city was distinctive, with its own special history and traditions, its own achievement, its characteristic physical beauties and attractions. The traveler could learn something new from each place he visited.

The location of Antioch, on one of the most important trade routes between the East and the Graeco-Roman world, had early brought it prosperity and a sophisticated culture; and its benign climate, tempered in summer by the breezes which daily blew up the valley of the Orontes River from the Mediterranean Sea, made it a popular vacation spot and summer refuge from the extremes of heat and dampness which prevailed elsewhere in the eastern Mediterranean region. Indeed it was not only at the season of the Olympic

CHAPTER I

"FAIR CROWN OF THE ORIENT"

"Orientis apicem pulcrum . . . ."
—AMMIANUS MARCELLINUS

IN July and August of every leap year in the Julian calendar, visitors journeyed to Antioch in Syria from all over the Graeco-Roman world. The immediate occasion of their coming was the quadrennial Olympic Games of Antioch, a festival which had been established in the Syrian capital as long ago as the time of Augustus (23 B.C.–A.D. 14) and Claudius (A.D. 41–54). These games had in fact by the reign of the Emperor Theodosius the Great (A.D. 379–95) become almost more famous than the original Olympic Games in Greece for which they were named. The festival offered something for everyone—athletic contests of all kinds, horse races, musical contests, declamations, and literary displays. Held in the rainless months when the summer weather was at its best, they had come to be a popular fixture in the world of that day.

But it was not always simply the games that attracted people to Antioch. The city was commonly held to be the finest in the Greek East—the historian Ammianus Marcellinus, himself an Antiochene, called it "the fair crown of the Orient"—and that meant that it ranked as one of the handsomest cities in the civilized world. In size and beauty, in the East, its only rivals were Alexandria and Constantinople. Athens, al-

ANTIOCH

In the Age of Theodosius the Great

Games that the city drew visitors to it; strangers arrived every day, and they always found a welcome and excellent food and lodging.

Whether one arrived from the seaport Seleucia Pieria, by the road which ran alongside the Orontes River, or came along the level road from Cilicia and Asia Minor, to the north, or followed the road from Beroea (modern Aleppo) and the east and south, the first sight of the city was the massive shape of Mount Silpius, towering above it. Fifteen hundred feet high at its highest point, the great mountain lay stretched out along the southern and eastern side of the city, like a giant shield protecting the city beneath it. As one drew nearer, one could see the line of walls which ran along the top of the mountain and descended its slopes at the northern and southern ends of the city, to continue across the level ground to the river. At the west, the Orontes formed the boundary of the city, flowing south toward Seleucia Pieria and the sea. The city, then, was an oblong, some two miles long and one mile wide, lying between river and mountain. In the river, at the northern part of the city, lay an island which began to be occupied as a part of the city as the population expanded under the Seleucid kings.

If the visitor were sufficiently energetic, he would make the ascent of Mount Silpius. This was by no means an easy undertaking, for the climb to the top of the mountain and the return journey would take a full day for most people. But the reward that awaited the climber was magnificent. Even if there had been no city at the foot of the mountain, there were not many places in which the summit of a mountain revealed scenery of such variety and splendor. South of Mount Silpius lay the mountain range running to the sea, with ridges and peaks culminating in the snow-capped Mount Casius on the coast. Through this range ran the thread of the Orontes River along its narrow valley. Across the Orontes from Mount Silpius the vast open plain opposite the city stretched west and north to the mountains which guarded the pass into Asia Minor. Turning to the side of the mountain away from the city, the visitor would see gently rolling country dotted with orchards. Such was the magnificent background for the history of Antioch.

In classical times, "history" was often conceived in terms of the histories of cities. The great cities of the Greek world, Athens, Alexandria, Antioch, Constantinople, all had their chroniclers. Local libraries and archives preserved the records and traditions of which the citizens were justly proud. Rivalries grew between cities as they did between states and nations in later times. There were a number of well-known works on Antioch which a traveler could read in preparation for his visit to the city. One of the best-known of these was *The Foundation of Antioch* by the celebrated writer Pausanias of Damascus. Histories of the Seleucid kings had been written by Euphorion of Chalcis, the learned librarian of King Antiochus the Great (224–187 B.C.) and by Nikolaos of Damascus. One of the most interesting books was the monograph *On the Festivals of Daphne*, written by Protagorides of Cyzicus in the reign of King Antiochus IV (176–146 B.C.) to celebrate the famous suburb Daphne, a few miles south of the city, which was one of the most beautiful spots in the ancient world, and a source of special pride and pleasure to the people of Antioch. The geographer Strabo, in his book which we can still read today, drew on the geographical treatise of the learned Posidonius of Apamea, which provided a great deal of information about Antioch.

In addition, the traveler in the time of Theodosius the Great would be able to read the brilliant new panegyric of the city by the famous writer Libanius of Antioch, which had made such a success when it was declaimed at the local Olympic Games a few years previously. Many critics considered this the most distinguished description of the city, and it was already being used as a model panegyric in the schools, not only in Antioch but elsewhere. It was especially admired for its descriptions of the natural beauties of Antioch and its vicinity.

A Hellenistic foundation, Antioch (unlike some of the older Greek cities) had enjoyed all the advantages of scientific city-planning. Among all the Hellenistic foundations, Antioch indeed was one of the most fortunate in its site. In classical city-planning and political economy the healthfulness of the site was the prime consideration in the choice of the location of a new city; for when the city was regarded as the indispensable center of civilization, it was on the physical advantages of the site that the success and prosperity of a city largely depended. Water supply, climate, and drainage were carefully studied, and the stress which Aristotle in his treatise on *Politics* laid on the water, the air, and the planning of the streets of a city reflects the extensive experience of the Greeks in establishing the new cities which their commercial growth and military conquests made necessary.

In all these respects Antioch could claim superiority. Situated in the prosperous northwestern corner of Syria, it lay a convenient distance—eighteen miles—from the sea, close enough for easy communication, and at the same time far enough away for safety in the event of enemy attack. The land all around Antioch was fertile, well watered, and well drained; and there were communications, long established and well known, both by land and along the river.

There had been Greek traders settled on the coast of Syria as far back as Mycenaean times, long before the foundation of Antioch, and the legends which the city cherished told how famous figures of mythology had visited the site of the future city, and had often settled there. It was by this means that the region had been marked out by the will of the gods as the site of a city.

The Argives under Triptolemus, searching for the wandering Io, had come to Mount Silpius and had been so smitten with the beauty of the place that they gave up their search and settled on the mountain. Later they were joined by settlers of noble lineage from Crete under the leadership of Kasos. Kasos later married the daughter of Salaminus, king of Cyprus, who brought companions with her to her new home. Then came the children of Herakles, driven into exile by Eurystheus. All this legendary history formed a noble lineage for the city.

In the local tradition, the mythological visitors were succeeded by Alexander the Great and his victorious army. The people of Antioch were proud to claim that after the battle of Issus, in the autumn of 333 B.C., in which the Persian host was defeated, Alexander with his army passed by the site of Antioch, on his way south to Palestine, and when he saw the spot, he vowed that he would found a city there when his campaigns were finished. The story related that Alexander drank the water of one of the local springs and declared that it was sweeter than his mother's milk. Whatever the truth of the tradition may be, the abundance and excellence of the water supply was undoubtedly one of the major factors in the decision to build a city on this spot. This part of Syria enjoys a special geological formation of fissured limestone containing underground caverns and reservoirs in which is collected the water that falls during the winter rainy season. Where faults in the limestone produce springs, the water flows at all seasons of the year, including the dry, hot summer. Thus there were perpetual springs everywhere in this neighborhood, notably in what became the suburb Daphne, five miles south of Antioch. Here at one point there are several large ever-flowing springs, close together, and since Daphne was at a higher level than Antioch, this water could easily be carried by gravity through an aqueduct to the city.

The actual founder of Antioch was Seleucus Nicator, "The Conqueror," a general of Alexander the Great's and one of the successors who divided the vast empire that Alexander had won. After Alexander's death Seleucus acquired Syria for his share; and whether or not he was carrying out a plan of Alexander's, he chose wisely when he founded Antioch in 300 B.C. Seleucus and his advisers had obviously considered the various possibilities, and it is evident that the site was laid out after careful study. While the water supply must have been one of the major attractions of the site, another factor which was clearly of importance was the temperate and healthful climate. Mild in the winter, with regularly recurring spells of sunshine during this rainy season, the climate during the long, dry summer was, for this part of the world, remarkably pleasant. A regular breeze blew daily from the sea up the Orontes Valley, and in the long summer months (May was already hot) this steady stream of fresh, cool air did much to relieve the high temperatures and dissipate the humidity. Antioch soon became a summer resort to which people came from the rest of Syria and from Palestine and Egypt. The care with which the much-prized air was studied and appreciated is shown by the fact that when the streets of the new city were laid out, on the gridiron pattern which had become established in city-planning, they were not planned in full geometrical relation with the river, but were laid out on a bias with the river, oriented carefully so that the main thoroughfares caught the breeze as it blew up the valley.

9

The natural beauty of the site was a final attraction. It would have been difficult to find elsewhere such a combination of natural advantages in a setting of scenic beauty provided by the mountain with its vast bulk and varied contours, by the sweeping view across the plain beyond the river, and by the gently rolling wooded ground between Antioch and the lovely plateau overlooking the Orontes, five miles south of the city, which became the celebrated suburb Daphne. The mountain was a source of constant pleasure to the eye. In the morning, its slope toward the city lay in shadow as the sun came up on the other side of the mountain, while the plain beyond was receiving the first rays of light. All day the colors of the rocks and scrub growth on the mountainside seemed to change with the changing light, and in the evening, as the sun went down, the slopes of the mountain still lay in sunlight when everything else below was growing dark.

By contrast with the mass of the mountain, the flat plain beyond the Orontes stretched for many miles west and north to a rim of hills and mountains. To the northwest ran the road to the Gulf of Issus, and on beyond to Tarsus and the Cilician Gates. This sweep of level plain served as a peculiarly effective setting for Mount Silpius.

In addition to such attractions, Seleucus Nicator and his advisers could see that the site offered important commercial and military advantages. Seleucus' purpose was to secure control of the northern and western part of Syria, and to this end he founded four "sister cities," named for members of his family. These were placed in two pairs, each consisting of seaport and inland city. The northern pair, Antioch with its seaport Seleucia, was matched to the south by Apamea, another inland city like Antioch, with its seaport Laodicea.

Seleucia was an important adjunct to Antioch, giving it

maritime communications without the unattractive features of life about a harbor. It was built on an impregnable acropolis at the mouth of the Orontes, with a good harbor which had been used by traders since early Greek days, long before the foundation of Antioch. Originally Seleucia had been intended as the capital of the Seleucid dynasty, but after Seleucus Nicator's death Antioch became the royal seat. The reasons for this were obvious. Its position in the road network of Syria gave it the control of all land traffic in that area. Antioch dominated both the north-south roads which joined Syria, Palestine, and Asia Minor, and the even more important east-west communications which ran from the desert and the Tigris-Euphrates Valley to the Mediterranean. The Orontes was navigable as far up as Antioch, and the city became the terminus of the caravan route from the east. Goods brought from Persia, India, and even China were unloaded from the camels at Antioch and placed in boats which descended the river to Seleucia, whence ships carried them all over the Mediterranean and to the Atlantic Coast ports. The same communications of course made the city a vital military center. The other foundations of Seleucus did not possess the same advantages, and Antioch inevitably became far more important than its neighbors.

Thus everything combined to give Antioch a unique place among the cities of Syria. From its political and commercial position came a material prosperity which distinguished Antioch at all periods of its history. The neighborhood itself was rich; orchards, fields, and forests provided an abundance of fruit and wheat; and there were vegetable gardens all about the city. Hunting was an important source of food, as well as a favorite sport. The forests provided timber for building, and stone could be quarried in the near-by mountains. One special source of enjoyment was the abundant supply of fish furnished by the Mediterranean, the Orontes, and the Lake of Antioch which lay in the plain north of the city.

Antioch and its sister cities had been intended, by their Graeco-Macedonian founders, as centers of Hellenic civilization in the Oriental lands which Alexander the Great had conquered. Greek cities were established in all the regions to which Alexander penetrated, and with the city—always regarded by the Greeks as the natural center of political and cultural life—came Greek education and social customs. Within less than a generation, the cities of Alexander and his successors created a new world for Greek civilization.

Among these new creations, Antioch was typical. Some of the original settlers were Macedonian soldiers, veterans of Seleucus' army; but there were also Athenian colonists, and one of the chief sources of pride of the people of Antioch was their descent from this ancient and famous Greek stock. In the Greek world, nothing could be more distinguished than Athenian ancestry, and it was to their Attic origin that the people of Antioch traced the greatness of their city.

But alongside the Hellenic settlers there was also the local element in the population, the indigenous Semitic-speaking people who before the coming of Alexander had been subjects of the Persian Empire. This native population would inevitably become one of the elements of the Seleucid realm, and Seleucus' plan for Antioch included a quarter for the native Syrians, separate from that of the Greeks and Macedonians.

While these two elements inevitably remained distinct throughout the city's history, their presence gave Antioch a special character as a center of commerce and culture which looked both to the East and to the West. As such the city could become at the same time the metropolis of Syria and a center of Hellenic civilization which was in close touch with Oriental culture. Oriental traders constantly visited the city and kept it in touch with the thought-world of the East.

Finally, there was a large and flourishing Jewish community, founded by veterans of Seleucus' armies who were given farms near Daphne as rewards for their services. This Jewish colony played an important part in the city's history.

Seleucus' first successors were worthy of the founder of their dynasty. Under them, as the royal residence, the city grew, and the successive kings adorned it with statues and public buildings, many of them still standing in Theodosius' day—notably some of the ancient temples, the library, and the council chamber. The gods, rightly worshiped, continued to be lovers of Antioch. As the city expanded, more settlers of Greek stock came to it—Aetolians, Cretans, and Euboeans. Adorned by the spoils of war, the city became one of the finest in the Greek world, distinguished by its learned philosophers and men of letters.

In time, and inevitably in the world of that day, the Seleucid dynasty declined in vigor. Rome was already becoming the dominant power in the eastern Mediterranean. The Seleucid kings, wholly occupied with dynastic quarrels and rivalries, steadily lost power and wealth; and eventually it became necessary, for the sake of order and security, for Rome to occupy Syria (64 B.C.).

Here there was the beginning of a new and vigorous element in the city's history. The Romans, in expanding eastward, respected the existing institutions and customs so far as possible. For Greek culture they had a deep respect, and nothing was done to its detriment. But Antioch was now the capital of the new Roman province of Syria, the seat of a Roman governor, Roman legions, and Roman businessmen; and the emperors beginning with Augustus determined to transform the city physically and make it worthy of its new role. The main street was lined with the famous double colonnades; temples to the Roman gods were built; a statue of the she-wolf with Romulus and Remus, symbol of the origin of Rome, was set up. For the official state cult, a statue of the goddess Roma was provided. The theatre was enlarged, and aqueducts and basilicas were built.

Distinguished as a Hellenistic capital, Antioch now entered a new career as the Graeco-Roman metropolis of Syria. The Latin language and literature took their place beside Greek—though never on quite the same footing—and the Roman governors and their suites added a new element to the culture of the city. One of many young Romans of prominent families who visited the city, Pliny the Younger served in Antioch as a junior officer at the beginning of his career. Antioch received many benefits from the philhellenic emperors who visited it, and under Roman protection the ancient Greek culture of the city continued to flourish while local orators, poets, and scholars continued to write in Greek. Libanius himself, though by no means friendly to Rome or to Latin civilization, wrote that the city prospered under its new rulers; and if it lived, inescapably, under an alien regime, it still was in direct touch with its Hellenic past.

Not much later than the Romans came Christianity, as the final and most important factor to shape the life and culture of the city. The story of the early mission to Antioch, where the disciples were first called Christians, was well known, and was indeed a unique source of pride to all Christians who later lived in Antioch.

The city was an ideal base for the mission to the Gentiles. The Roman authorities could keep better order in Antioch than they could in Jerusalem, and the missionaries had not to fear the attacks of fanatical Jews. In the cosmopolitan society of Antioch both classical and Oriental cults were familiar, and in a city which was in constant contact with the East, new religious ideas were not a novelty. Perhaps the chief local factor which smoothed the way for Christianity at Antioch was that numbers of Gentiles, dissatisfied with the traditional pagan cults, had been attracted to the Jewish synagogues, where the books of the Old Testament, read and expounded in Greek translation, offered a moral and ethical teaching which many found far superior to anything that paganism could provide. These Gentile visitors to the synagogues did not become Jews, for conversion would mean renunciation of nationality and cultural heritage; but when the Christian preachers came they found many people who were already familiar with those aspects of their teaching which were based on the Old Testament, and it was undoubtedly the Gentiles acquainted with the Septuagint, the Old Testament in Greek, who furnished many of the early converts in the days of Paul, Barnabas, and Peter, who was recorded as the first bishop of Antioch.

With such a beginning Antioch, with its excellent communications by land and sea, served as an ideal base for the missionary journeys of Paul and his companions. The people of the city could feel that outside of Jerusalem itself no community had played such a part in the earliest beginnings of Gentile Christianity.

CHAPTER II

A TOUR OF THE CITY

"This city is like no other."

—LIBANIUS

A S he set out on his initial tour of the city, the visitor would very likely be conducted along the route described in Libanius' celebrated encomium of Antioch. This had the advantage of offering a systematic view of the whole city, followed by a tour of the suburb Daphne, ending at the famous springs. Libanius' encomium comprised a description of the foundation of Antioch by Seleucus the Conqueror, and an account of its institutions and culture, closing with the description of the city and Daphne. The work was considered to be one of Libanius' masterpieces, and it soon became a classic. Illustrated editions of it were published, depicting scenes of the itinerary as the orator described them. A century later, a wealthy householder at Daphne had one of the main rooms of his villa decorated with a mosaic floor whose border reproduced in the same order many of the scenes in Libanius' itinerary. This mosaic, preserved in part and recovered in 1932, gives a precious glimpse of the life of Antioch, and combined with the more detailed text of Libanius, it furnishes us with a picture of the monuments of Antioch, and of life in the city, such as we possess for no other place at that time.

The visitor—following this itinerary—would come first to

the heavily fortified gate in the northern wall of the city, on the road which led from Beroea. The roadway, thirty feet wide, was paved with massive blocks of Egyptian granite. As he passed through the monumental entrance with its heavy doors, he found himself in the main thoroughfare of the city, its granite roadway flanked on either side by covered colonnades, each, like the open street, thirty feet wide.

Running through the long axis of the city, north and south, the main street was two miles long. This famous thoroughfare, resembling the colonnaded street at Palmyra, was one of the city's greatest sources of pride, and one of the well-known reasons for its fame. The wide roadway provided ample room for the busy traffic of the city, and the spacious sidewalks on either side of it, each lined with two rows of columns, provided pleasant accommodation for pedestrians and loungers. The colonnades were two-storied and roofed, with stairs at intervals leading up to the second-story galleries and the roofs. Under the colonnades there was shade in the summer and shelter from rain and snow in the winter. Along the inner sides of the colonnades ran the walls of houses and public buildings, their entrances opening between the columns, while on the side toward the street merchants and vendors often set up booths between the columns. The municipal authorities found it difficult to control these intrusions.

The street had been built under the auspices of the Emperors Augustus (23 B.C.–A.D. 14) and Tiberius (A.D. 14–37), with assistance from King Herod, at the time when the Romans were transforming Hellenistic Antioch into a Roman city. In Hellenistic times this had been a graveled roadway running along the outside of Seleucus' city, but with the growth of Antioch it had become the principal thoroughfare.

The roadway was open to the sky, but since it ran north and south it was shaded during part of the day, and it caught the breeze which blew up the Orontes Valley in the summer. It was full of the most varied traffic. Travelers on horseback or in carriages drawn by mules; donkeys heavily loaded with burdens of all kinds, singly or in strings, led by drivers armed with sticks; two-wheeled carts carrying building materials; porters bearing heavy loads—every kind of activity could be seen in this thoroughfare and the side streets which opened from it. Some drivers, in order to escape the sun, led their asses and camels through the porticoes—"as though they were brides," as someone said. Farmers brought food into the city in carts or on donkeys, and the municipal authorities forced them to carry rubbish out of the city as they left. Women hurried on errands, their children trailing behind them. Boys walked to school, chaperoned by slaves carrying their books and wax writing tablets secured in leather straps. High officials and army officers passed on horseback, their harness and uniforms glittering. Wealthy citizens had the harness of their horses inlaid with gold, and ladies went about the city in brightly painted wooden carriages. An important personage, seated in aloof dignity on his white horse, would have a servant armed with a stick running before him, shouting and clearing the way through the crowd for his illustrious master. Many of the great houses of the city had Negro servants whose liveries were trimmed with gold. The governors of Syria, the Counts of the East, and the generals of the eastern command when they appeared in public were escorted by detachments of the archers who served as police.

The streets and the open squares which occurred at intervals throughout the city exhibited all the varied activity of a Mediterranean city, where in the warm, dry summer, life was largely lived out of doors. Antioch was not like other cities in which the vendors of different types of goods tended to congregate, so that each commodity could be purchased in only one part of the city. Thus one would buy hardware in one section of the city, leather in another, cloth in a third region. Instead, Libanius tells us, everything in Antioch was sold in all parts of the city, and people did not have to make long expeditions in order to make their purchases. The shopper could go from shop to shop, or find an open square filled with the bustle of buying and selling in the open air.

The squares served as social centers as well. Citizens paced about in twos and threes, conversing, while children played tug of war, falling backward sometimes as their rope broke in the middle. Beggars danced and piped, and jugglers and acrobats wandered about giving performances wherever they could collect a crowd. Philosophers made their way about, distinguished by the recognized signs of their calling, the long beard (most men were clean shaven), the threadbare cloak, and the staff carried in the right hand. The streets and market places were busy until midnight, and Antioch enjoyed public street lighting, an unusual thing in those days.

There were camps all about Antioch, which had a permanent garrison and was headquarters for the defense of the Persian frontier; and soldiers were to be seen everywhere in the streets dressed in their uniforms tunics and kilts, with their branch of service—artillery, cavalry, infantry—indicated by the color of their uniforms. All through the slow-moving crowds one could see visitors from remote parts of the empire or from foreign lands, easily identified by their exotic dress. Servants and porters hurried along, balancing bundles on their heads; and men often carried lumber and other heavy burdens, for it could be cheaper to hire a man than to employ an animal.

At the public fountains at the corners of the streets women

and children filled tall earthenware water jars, which they carried on the shoulder, balanced with one hand, or on the back, the pointed bottom of the jar resting in a sling which passed around the forehead and down the back. With the abundant water supply of Antioch, there was no quarreling and pushing about the fountains, as there was in some other cities where water was scarce and the supply irregular. Indeed, many of the large private houses in Antioch had water piped into their courtyards from the aqueducts.

Dress had not changed essentially for many generations and would not change for many more. Men customarily wore a one-piece tunic reaching to the knees, and belted at the waist, to give the effect of a kilt. This was of wool in the winter, cotton or linen in the summer. Officials and citizens of substance wore in addition robes reaching to the ground. In winter there would be worn a wool cloak with an attached hood. While workmen and slaves were barefooted, most men who could do so wore sandals, with tight woolen trousers in cold weather. Officials and army officers wore distinctive cloaks as part of their uniform, fastened at the shoulder with ornamental brooches which betokened rank—officers' cloaks were white. The uniform belt was worn as a badge of service in the army or the civil service.

Women wore long robes reaching to the ground, of various colors and materials—wool, linen, silk—depending on the season of the year and the occasion and status of the wearer. Outdoors the hair was covered with a colored scarf. In winter there would be a wool cloak with a hood. Children wore smaller counterparts of their parents' clothing, and carried toys which have been familiar at all times—wooden or rag dolls, hoops, tops.

The long line of the main street was broken at regular intervals by side streets, on one side running up toward the mountain, on the other side across the level area toward the river. Only the more important of these side streets were colonnaded. The city-blocks were of uniform size, about one hundred yards long and half as wide. The lower slopes of the mountain provided choice sites for houses; Libanius wrote of the pleasures of living in this area:

> The mountain rises up, stretched out beside the city like a shield raised high in defense, and the last dwellers on the lower slopes of the mountain have nothing to fear from the heights, but they have the sources of every happiness, springs, plants, gardens, breezes, flowers, the songs of birds, and the enjoyment of spring earlier than the others have it.

Fine villas lined the slopes, with their dining rooms arranged so that guests could enjoy the view over the city.

As he passed along the street the visitor would see ahead of him a distant vista of an open plaza in the middle of which stood a column bearing a statue of the Emperor Tiberius. At this point the direction of the street changed very slightly, so that as one walked along the avenue toward the center of the city, from either direction, one's view came to rest upon an architectural composition, a more pleasing effect than a straight, unending row of colonnades disappearing into the distance would have been.

When he came to this square, the visitor would pause. He was in the center of the city. On his right, at right angles to the main street, he saw a colonnaded street leading to the river and the large island in the Orontes. At the head of this street, all along the side of the plaza, stood a handsome *nymphaeum*, consisting of an ornamental façade of variegated marble and colored mosaic faced with columns between which were fountains enclosed in niches. The water ran out into a marble basin paved with mosaic.

To the visitor's left, a short colonnaded street, running in the direction of the mountain, led to the recently completed Forum named for Theodosius' predecessor, the Emperor Valens (A.D. 364–78), on which stood some of the most important public buildings in the city.

As he walked up the sloping street and entered the forum with its gleaming marble buildings, the visitor would see about him the tokens of all the varied activities which went to make up the life of the city. Government, social life, religion, and trade were all represented in this splendid composition of monumental public buildings grouped about a vast open area. The forum was a distinctively Roman institution, taking the place of the agora or market place of the Greeks, such as the two old agoras in Antioch which had been the centers of the city's life in the days of the Seleucids. The Forum of Valens at Antioch was intended to be one of the most magnificent in the Graeco-Roman world, resembling in its general composition the Forum of Trajan in Rome.

There were splendid buildings already in existence which Valens' architects could use as the basis for the new forum; indeed the monumental development of the area went back to the time of Julius Caesar and before. The oldest buildings in this part of the city were the Temple of Ares and the Temple of Athene, which were of Hellenistic date, the Temple of Ares having originally had a large enclosure in which religious rites connected with the army had been performed. Near by was a basilica called the Caesarium, built by Julius Caesar, on the plan of a similar building which he had presented to the city of Alexandria. The distinctive feature of this was an open court with a vaulted apse in front of which stood two statues, one of the Fortune of Rome, the other of Caesar. The Emperor Trajan (A.D. 98–117) had added a monumental arch. The Emperor Commodus (A.D. 180–92)

22

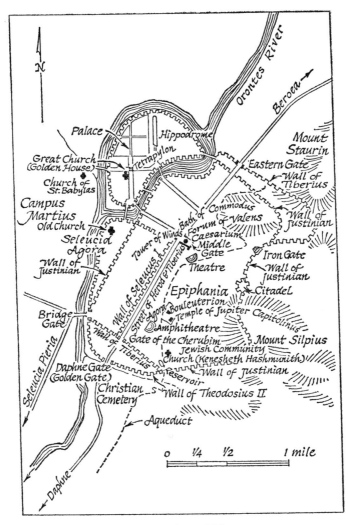

ANTIOCH
Restored as of the Age of Theodosius the Great

had done much to beautify the area; here he had built two exercise grounds for use in the local Olympic Games, called the Xystos and the Plethrion, and he had erected a temple to Olympian Zeus, the patron deity of the games. He had also restored the old Temple of Athene. Near Commodus' buildings stood the Tower of the Winds, built by the Emperor Vespasian (A.D. 69–79), which contained the Horologion, a public clock.

When Valens had decided to turn this area into a forum, the necessary open space was obtained by demolishing part of the Caesarium and by building vaults over the stream Parmenius, which flowed from the mountain to the river through this area. The open area, paved with marble, was surrounded on its four sides by colonnades, decorated with coffered ceilings, mosaics, and paintings. The columns were of marble brought from Salona, and statues stood at intervals around the porticos. Opposite the Bath of Commodus, which had been turned into the headquarters of the Governor of Syria, Valens had built a new basilica. A *macellum* or provisions market took up some of the former space of the Temple of Ares. The forum contained three statues of the Emperor Valentinian I (A.D. 364–75), one on a column in the middle of the open space, the other two in different parts of the Caesarium. Nearby Valens built a *kynegion* or amphitheatre for shows and combats of wild beasts and gladiators. The number and variety of the buildings in this part of the city meant that at all hours of the day one would find in the forum a varied collection of people intent on business of every kind.

The visitor, having seen the forum and its neighborhood, would set out for the island along the transverse colonnaded street. Along this, the distance from the main street to the river was about one-third of a mile. On reaching the Orontes the visitor would cross a stone bridge and find himself on the island, one of the old quarters of the city, surrounded by its own wall and linked by five bridges to the mainland part of the city and to the plain on the far side of the Orontes.

As in the main part of the city, the streets on the island were laid out on the gridiron pattern, with two main streets crossing at right angles in the center of the island. At their junction the visitor would come to a square from which the four branches of the streets set out to the four quarters of the compass, the beginnings of the streets marked by four monumental arches on the sides of the square.

The island exhibited a concentration of buildings of special interest—the principal church of the city, the imperial palace, the hippodrome. The church was the famous octagonal "Golden House" built by Constantine the Great in honor of the city where the disciples had first been called Christians. Standing in an open court surrounded by colonnades, the octagon with its gilded dome towered above the other buildings on the island and could be seen from all parts of the city. The church itself was built of rich marbles, and the interior was decorated with mosaics, statues, and lamps of silver and bronze. The Eucharistic vessels on the altar were of gold, replacing the original vessels presented by Constantine and his son Constantius, which had been carried off when the pagan Emperor Julian closed the church. This was the cathedral seat of the Bishop of Antioch, and when church councils were convened at Antioch it was here that they met, in the church in the winter and in the cool colonnades around the courtyard in the summer. The church stood on the site of an old public bath which had fallen into disrepair and had been demolished to make way for the new cathedral. The construction had been in charge of Plutarchus, the first Christian governor of Syria. The building had not been finished at the time of Constantine's death in A.D. 337, and was completed by his son and successor Constantius. The unusual octagonal plan was later employed in the Church of St. Symeon Stylites in the hilly country between Antioch and Beroea. A metrical inscription in Greek commemorated the construction:

For Christ did Constantine make this lovely dwelling,
In all respects like the shining vaults of Heaven.
Constantius his son obeyed the commands of the ruler;
The Count Gorgonius oversaw the construction.

The walled enclosure around the church contained residences for the clergy, a *xenon* or guest-house for travelers, schools, and kitchens for feeding the poor of the city.

Near the church, on the outer edge of the island, stood the great palace, built by Diocletian (before A.D. 298) for the use of the emperors when they visited the city. The entrance was approached along a short colonnaded street forming part of the symmetrical plan of the streets of the island. The rectangular plan of this palace was later repeated in the one which Diocletian built for himself at Spalato on the Adriatic Coast. Others of the same plan were to be seen at Thessalonica and Constantinople. This palace plan was based on the standard plan of the fortified camps which were regularly constructed by the Roman army, divided into four sections by two streets crossing one another at right angles. The great structure was filled with a vast complex of living apartments, baths, a church, quarters for servants and soldiers, and an oval riding track, hedged with evergreens, on which the emperor could take his exercise. The palace occupied nearly a quarter of the island. Libanius wrote that it was "divided into so many chambers and porticoes and halls that even those who are well accustomed to it become lost as they go from door to door." The outer wall of the complex ran along the river, and there a covered and sheltered portico built on top of the wall provided a walk for the emperor from which he could look out over the river and the plain beyond it to the mountains in the distance.

Beside the palace stood the hippodrome which, with its arena over 1,600 feet long, was one of the largest in the Roman world. This dated to the time of the Roman occupation of Syria. The location of the chief church and the hippodrome near the palace symbolized the different aspects of the emperor's functions which were expressed by his ceremonial appearances at the great services of the church and his presence as presiding figure at the chariot races in the hippodrome, which were provided by the state for the enjoyment of the people. The same conjunction of palace, principal church, and hippodrome could be seen in the capital, Constantinople.

In the remainder of the island one could see luxurious villas and visit great public baths with their succession of pools and chambers for the various stages of bathing and recreation, the halls all richly ornamented with architectural moldings, sculptures, variegated marbles, and mosaic floors which were cool and pleasant in the summer. The baths were surrounded by gardens and open exercise grounds.

But the visitor had still seen only half the city. Returning by another bridge to the mainland, he would find himself on the bank of the river, in the oldest part of Antioch. Here on the edge of the water, behind the wall which ran along the Orontes, was the original settlement of Seleucus the Conqueror. The original agora or market place had lain along the river where boats and barges could discharge their cargoes at stone quays. Here too were the original temples and government buildings of Seleucid times. There had been no Seleucid palace, for the Hellenistic kings had been content to live in large and luxurious versions of the private houses of the time. In this quarter stood the Old Church, supposed to date from apostolic times, and it was in this part of the city that St. Paul had preached, in the street called Singon Street, near the Pantheon.

The old quarter of the city exhibited temples and statues which went back to the earliest history of Antioch and recalled to the visitor the stories about the foundation of the city. There was the ancient Temple of Zeus, founded by Seleucus the Conqueror as a thank-offering to the guardian deity of the Seleucid house, for his favor and for his approval of the establishment of the city. This stood on the original agora or market place of Antioch, which covered the area of more than four city blocks.

There were several famous statues. One was the bronze figure of Athene which Seleucus had erected for the religious needs of the Athenians whom he had brought to settle in his new city. But the most famous was the statue of the Tyche or Good Fortune of Antioch, which had been executed at Seleucus' order by Eutychides of Sicyon, a pupil of the celebrated sculptor Lysippus. This statue had become the ancestor of many personifications of Good Fortune which were set up throughout the cities of the Greek-speaking world; and from being a symbol of prosperity and good luck, these Tyches became the personifications of their cities.

The Tyche of Antioch, the first such figure to be created, was of bronze, as was appropriate for a statue which was to stand out of doors. It showed the goddess, draped in a long robe, seated on a rock, with one knee crossed over the other. With her left hand she supported herself on the rock; in her right she held a sheaf of wheat, symbolizing the material prosperity of the city. The rock represented Mount Silpius;

and beneath the feet of the goddess was the figure of a nude youth, his arms extended in the motion of swimming. This figure personified the Orontes River. On her head the Tyche wore a turreted crown representing the crenelated city wall. The statue was raised on a pedestal and sheltered under an ornamental roof supported on four columns, one at each corner. Miniature copies of the Tyche were made as souvenirs and sold to visitors.

Returning to the main street, the visitor would pass into Epiphania, the quarter built by King Antiochus IV, surnamed Epiphanes (174-164 B.C.), one of the last of the great Seleucid rulers. This section of the city, lying between the main street and the mountain, had been settled by the overflow of the population when the city began to outgrow its original quarters. Some people had thought that Antiochus Epiphanes was a madman; others, that he was a genius. Whatever its source may have been, his passion for building was famous; indeed, this was one of the ways an ancient ruler could perpetuate his name. He built many things throughout his kingdom and even beyond, and he made his new quarter of Antioch one of the most beautiful parts of the city.

There was a new agora, built to relieve the old agora near the river of some of its business. One of the most famous of Antiochus' buildings stood on the agora, the *bouleuterion* or council chamber, which resembled the one at Miletus. This was still in use for the meetings of the senate of Antioch in Theodosius' day. There was also the famous Temple of Jupiter Capitolinus, the leading Roman deity, built as a compliment to the Romans whom Antiochus much admired.

Other monuments left by Antiochus Epiphanes were a new aqueduct tunneled into the side of the mountain, bringing water from Daphne, the work of the Roman engineer

Cossutius; and the Charonion, a gigantic head carved in the rock on the side of the mountain above the city as an apotropaic talisman during a visitation of the plague. This bust continued to look down over the city throughout its whole history, and the traveler was told various legends concerning it, not all of which could have been true.

One landmark in Antiochus' new quarter which every visitor had to see was the theatre, built at a spot where the slope of the mountain provided a natural curve for the accommodation of the hemicycle of marble seats. There were many statues around the entrances and along the front of the stage, chief among them—standing against the marble background of the stage—a figure of Calliope, the Muse who was regarded, along with Zeus and Apollo, as a tutelary deity of Antioch. Her temple, in the central part of the city, was one of the most important in Antioch. In the theatre she presided over the literary exhibitions which were regularly presented before the public there. The statue had been set up by the Emperor Trajan when he had enlarged the theatre to accommodate the growing population of the city. The figure was of gilded bronze and depicted Calliope in the style of the Tyche of Antioch, being crowned by Seleucus the Conqueror and his son Antiochus—the presence of the two kings typifying the honor which had been paid to Calliope at Antioch since the earliest history of the city.

Making his way south, toward the gate that led to Daphne, the visitor would pass the quarter where the Jewish community at Antioch had lived since Seleucus' reign. Here, on the side of the mountain, there was a famous church which had originally been the Kenesheth Hashmunith, the synagogue which was reputed to contain the tombs of the Maccabean martyrs. The priest Eleazer, the seven Maccabean brothers, and their mother all had died as martyrs for their faith in the warfare between Antiochus Epiphanes and his Jewish subjects in Palestine. The relics of these noble victims had been deeply venerated by the Jews, and in time, as Jewish conceptions of martyrdom had an important influence on Christian ideas, the synagogue had been converted into a church. There was some uncertainty as to the location of the relics, and according to another tradition they were preserved at Modeim in Palestine.

Another landmark in this part of the city was the Gate of the Cherubim, the southern gate of the city on the road that led to Daphne. Here the Emperor Titus, after the destruction of Jerusalem in A.D. 70, had set up, on the road outside the gate, bronze figures that were supposed to represent the Cherubim taken from the demolished Temple. Of course the original figures of the Cherubim no longer existed, but these were either an imitation of them or winged figures that could be called Cherubim. Over the gate Titus set up a figure of the Moon, which, with the Sun, was one of the representations of eternity in the imperial symbolism of that period.

At the gate the visitor would see all the familiar figures that characteristically clustered about the entrance to a large city. A detachment of soldiers stood guard. There were beggars, loungers, and vendors of souvenirs; and a regular little market had grown up, peopled with sellers of fish, meat, fruit, bread, and other kinds of food, as well as cool drinks. Each man stood behind his little portable table, which he could carry suspended by a strap around his neck, and cried out his wares. Children played in the dust, and dogs wandered about looking for scraps.

As he set out on the road to Daphne, five miles south of the city, the visitor passed on his left the oldest Christian cemetery of Antioch, a much-venerated spot which preserved the tombs of some of the best-known figures in the history of the Christian community. Buried there was St. Ignatius, the martyr-bishop of Antioch who was arrested in the time of the Emperor Trajan and sent to Rome, where he was executed by being eaten alive by wild beasts in the arena. His bones had been collected by the faithful in Rome and were later returned to Antioch for burial in the cemetery. Here too had been the tomb of St. Babylas, the bishop who was a martyr in the persecution under the Emperor Decius (A.D. 249–51). Under Gallus Caesar (A.D. 351–54) his body had been transferred to Daphne in an effort to put a stop to the oracle of Apollo there. A martyrium or martyr's shrine was built for him, and the presence of the saint's remains did inhibit the oracle; and so the pagan Emperor Julian (A.D. 361–63) had the body returned to the cemetery. Soon after Theodosius had come to the throne, Bishop Meletius had built a cruciform church in honor of St. Babylas across the Orontes, and the saint's remains finally came to rest there. There were many other tombs of local martyrs and holy men and women in the cemetery, and the Christian visitor would find there many objects of prayer and devotion.

The walk to Daphne was one of the special pleasures of the people of Antioch. As soon as one passed through the city gate one found oneself among the charms of nature. The road at first followed the left bank of the river, and there, on the left of the road, one found a succession of orchards and gardens filled with roses and other flowers. Here and there, surrounded by trees and flowers, stood a country villa belonging to one of the wealthy citizens. The road gradually turned away from the river and slowly began to climb, for Daphne was higher than Antioch. Now, on both sides of the road one came upon vineyards and handsome houses. Everywhere there were gardens filled with the roses used in making the perfume for which Antioch was famous. At intervals the road crossed a small stream flowing down from the mountainside to the Orontes, and there were springs beside the road at which the traveler could pause for a drink of the water which had a characteristic and agreeable flavor given to it by the limestone rock in which it had been stored in natural underground pools.

All along the road stood inns which tempted the traveler to pause and rest. These were sometimes one-storied, with a porch running across the front, sometimes of two stories, with a balcony built out from the façade of the upper level. On the grounds of the inns there were arbors formed of grape vines or rose bushes trained over trellises, forming outdoor dining rooms. The visitor could sit at a table or recline on a straw mat spread on the ground, as he chose. Refreshments were simple—the local wine mixed with cool water, or lemon or orange juice served in water which had been cooled in an underground cellar or drawn directly from a cold spring. For those who desired something more substantial, there were pastries and fruit. The shade was always cool, and one could watch the tops of the trees as they blew in the wind which came up the river valley.

As one approached Daphne the villas became more numerous, and one soon found oneself in the famous pleasure spot. Daphne was in some ways even better known than Antioch, and the city was sometimes known as "Antioch near Daphne." The region had a famous legendary history. It was reputed to have been founded by Herakles (an old name of the region was Herakleis), and Antioch took pride in the local legend that the Judgment of Paris, when Paris had had to decide which was most beautiful among the three goddesses—Hera, Athene, and Aphrodite—had taken place at Daphne.

The central part of the suburb was like any small town.

There was a market place with public baths and temples, and the streets, laid out on a regular plan, were filled with spacious houses. At the southern end of the suburb one came to the greatest sights of this lovely spot—the ever-flowing springs, the ruins of the Temple of Apollo which stood just below them, the theatre, and the Olympic stadium.

The Temple of Apollo, built by Seleucus the Conqueror, had been burned in the reign of the Emperor Julian, and now only its columns and parts of its walls were standing. Daphne had been dedicated to Apollo, as Antioch was to Zeus. It was here, according to legend, that Apollo had pursued the maiden Daphne, and that the maiden, to save herself from the god, was transformed into a laurel tree, which then became known by her name, *daphnê*. The very tree into which the maiden had been changed was shown to visitors. In his disappointment—the story went—the god discharged all of his arrows from his bow. Then one day, after Seleucus had founded Antioch, the King was hunting on this spot, and his horse pawed the earth and revealed a golden arrowhead. This was shown by the god's name inscribed on it to have been the property of Apollo, and thus the King was given a plain sign that the spot was to be sacred to the god. When he ordered the construction of the temple below the springs, Seleucus also planted the grove of cypress trees which became famous throughout the ancient world.

The springs were named Castalia, Pallas, and Saramanna. An oracle of Apollo had resided in the spring of Castalia. Flowing out of a cliff on one side of the plateau of Daphne, these springs had been beautified by successive rulers. The water, flowing perpetually from its underground natural reservoirs, gave this part of Daphne a freshness and coolness such as could be found nowhere else. The water was caught in large basins constructed of stone and then distributed through aqueducts to Daphne and carried along the mountainside to Antioch.

The most elaborate installation at the springs had been designed by the Emperor Hadrian (A.D. 117–38), who at Saramanna, one of the largest of the springs, had constructed an ornamental reservoir, semicircular at one end, containing rows of seats surmounted by a colonnaded promenade, where people could sit or walk about and enjoy the sound of the water and its coolness. At the point where the water entered the basin of the reservoir Hadrian constructed a temple in honor of the Nymphs who inhabited the springs. In the temple the Emperor placed a statue of himself as Zeus, seated and holding the celestial sphere.

The theatre had been built by the Emperor Titus with funds from the sale of the spoils of Jerusalem. It contained a statue of Titus' father the Emperor Vespasian, as well as many other ornamental statues which stood along the front of the stage.

What was in some ways almost the most famous monument in Daphne was the stadium used for the Olympic Games. There were twin towers beside the entrance, and within the stadium there was a Temple of Olympian Zeus, as well as a shrine of Nemesis placed in the curved end where the judges and other officials of the games sat.

Daphne was full of interest. There was an underground shrine of Hecate, reached by 365 steps. There were numerous inns and open colonnades in which one could find refreshments of all kinds. The Christian visitor would stop at the workshops of the martyrium of St. Babylas, where religious souvenirs were made for sale to travelers. One could also admire the imperial palace—smaller than that at Antioch—which had been built by the Emperor Diocletian. Above the walls of the houses along the streets one could see the tops of

the trees with which the gardens and courtyards were ornamented. From the most fortunate of these villas there was
a wide sweeping view across the valley of the Orontes to
the mountains on the other side of the river, and during the
daylight hours the view was constantly animated as the trees
swayed in the wind. It was no wonder that the wealthy
families of Antioch had their summer villas here.

Daphne was supremely an embodiment of the rich tradition of the classical world. Its natural beauty, carefully preserved and thoughtfully enhanced, was justly appreciated as
a setting for gods and goddesses. A place as beloved by the
divinities as Daphne must needs possess sovereign powers
for the human race, whose culture had been built up around
the stories of the gods and goddesses; and if there were villas
in Daphne which were frankly designed for the enjoyments
in which the pagan world took pleasure, it was also true
that the whole atmosphere of such a spot must also bring
a milder and more benign satisfaction and refreshment to
many of those whose good fortune it was to visit it. The
sober guest would find repose, delight, and healing in this
cool and quiet spot. No one reared in the classical tradition
could see Daphne without perceiving its beauty in the terms
of the classical literature which had been created and transmitted by men who wrote of the divinities who were thought
to have dwelt in such a spot.

By the time of the Christian Emperor Theodosius, of
course, literal belief in the ancient deities was no longer universal and accepted; but the culture was still a living force,
and Libanius and his friends who felt the power of this culture also felt a special power in Daphne. Thus at the close
of his description of Daphne, Libanius put into words what
every citizen of the classical world would feel there:

When a man sees this he cannot but cry out and leap for joy

and skip and clap his hands and bless himself for seeing the sight, and, so to speak, soar on wings of pleasure. One thing from one side and one thing from another enchants and astonishes; one thing holds one and another tears one away, and there pours upon the beholder's eyes an arresting brightness, the Temple of Apollo, the Temple of Zeus, the Olympic stadium, the theatre which furnishes every pleasure, the number and thickness and height of the cypresses, the shady paths, the choruses of singing birds, the even breeze, the odors sweeter than spices, the stately aqueducts, the vines trained to form banqueting halls—these are the gardens of Alcinous . . . the horn of Amaltheia, a veritable Sybaris. No matter what bath you choose before the others to bathe in, you will overlook a more delightful one. The place is so helpful to the body that, if you leave after even a brief stay, you will go away healthier than when you came; and if you were asked by what you were the most pleased, you would be at a loss for an answer, for it is to such a degree as this that every pleasure in Daphne rivals every other pleasure. No suffering is so powerful or so unconquerable or so long-standing that Daphne cannot drive it out, but as soon as you come to the place, the pain disappears. If the gods ever really leave heaven and come to earth, I believe that they must come together and hold their councils here, since they could not spend their time in a fairer place.

CHAPTER III

THE CHRISTIAN ROMAN EMPIRE

"God appointed Constantine . . . ."

—EUSEBIUS

THE visitor, whether he was a pagan or a Christian, knew that Antioch was at once an ancient pagan city and an important Christian community. Like everyone in the empire, he also knew, and had himself witnessed, the changes that had been taking place both in the structure of state and society and within the church.

The history of every family in Antioch had been affected in some way by the changes that had come about in the empire during the past three generations. These changes and developments concerned the whole of the empire; but Antioch, because of its geographical position and its administrative function, had witnessed these events more closely, and had suffered from some of them more severely, than many other cities.

It was not much more than one hundred years since Antioch had been captured and burned by the Persians. At that time the empire had been in very grave danger of breaking up, and for a while Antioch had actually been occupied by the troops of the desert kingdom of Palmyra. But fortune had been reversed, and there had appeared three emperors, Aurelian (A.D. 270–75), Diocletian (A.D. 284–305), and Constantine the Great (A.D. 306–37), who had succeeded in saving and transforming the state. It had been a radical transformation—as indeed it had to be—and every household in Antioch, rich and poor, had been touched by it. Now, in the time of Theodosius, things were better. There was external security, and there seemed no prospect of a return of the catastrophes of the days before Diocletian. But the citizens of Antioch under Theodosius had heard from their parents and their grandparents of all that had had to be done to save the state. Antioch seemed to have been as much changed, in the past few generations, as it had been when the last Seleucid kings had exhausted their powers and the Romans had found it necessary to take over Syria.

There were two developments at work simultaneously, the two combining to make the fourth century what has been called a "new-old" century. One set of factors was bringing about the decline of the pagan Roman state, while other forces were building up, out of this decaying world, the new Christian Roman Empire. Everything was being made new; politics, economics, religion, and intellectual life were all being put on a new and different basis.

The end of the classical imperial government had begun to be manifest during the crisis which had come upon the empire in the third century. A variety of practical factors were at work which combined to bring the state into real peril. Some of them reached far back into history. There had been for many years a decrease in the population—especially the free-born population—which brought a decline in man power which could not be arrested or reversed. By cutting down the supply of young men, this loss in population both weakened the army and caused a serious decline in agriculture and economic production. The loss in agriculture itself tended to perpetuate the decrease in the population. The land all this time lost in productivity.

The army, forced to reduce its numbers and to depend more and more on foreign mercenaries, found itself increasingly unequal to its duty of defending the long frontiers of the empire. Stretching from Britain and the Rhine along the Danube, the Black Sea and the mountains of Armenia to Mesopotamia, these boundaries were under steadily growing pressure from the barbarian tribes who sought to force their way into the empire in order to enjoy the prosperity and comforts of Roman civilization. The barbarians themselves had been forced out of their homes by the pressure of other nations who were making their way out of Asia, and they moved along the frontiers of the empire, now poorly fortified and poorly manned, looking for weak spots.

On the eastern frontier the problem was especially grave. Here the power of Persia was rising into a state which in many respects could consider itself a rival to the empire. The rich cities of Syria—before all, Antioch—offered wonderful loot, and when the Persians made their raids they carried off not only treasures but human captives as well. The desert defenses were extremely difficult to maintain, and the imperial troops could not keep out the raiders who moved so swiftly. Antioch itself was captured, burned, and occupied briefly in the middle of the third century. The invaders were aided by a pro-Persian party in the city, formed of people who had become so gravely dissatisfied with the imperial government that even the Persians seemed superior as an alternative.

Faced with these formidable problems, the Roman government proved itself unable to deal with the crisis; and there was a succession of weak emperors who either fought among themselves for power or failed to deal with the military problems to which their forces were unequal.

It seemed certain, indeed, that the state would have gone

under if there had not appeared the three emperors of exceptional gifts who were able, first, to put a stop to the military crisis and then to conceive and execute a massive reorganization not only of the state but of society. These gifted sovereigns—Aurelian, Diocletian, Constantine—planned a series of reforms in the government, the army, and the economic system which were designed to strengthen all aspects of the empire's life and work; and considering the weakness of the state as they found it, their efforts were remarkably successful.

In keeping with the ideas of politics and economics then current, the whole tendency of the reforms was to create an authoritarian state. The army was enlarged and reorganized into two parts, a frontier garrison force and a mobile field army, and the prestige and power of the military service were greatly enhanced. The emperor in his outward dress and surroundings became a military commander. Provinces were divided into smaller units and were grouped into new prefectures or geographical divisions which made for more efficient administration. The bureaucracy was enlarged and organized on a military basis, with the functionaries wearing uniforms. Under Constantine the capital was transferred from Rome to a new foundation, Constantinople—"Constantine's City"—which was better situated for military and administrative communications.

To save the economy and assure production, workers were "frozen" in their occupations, and production and commerce were controlled, in part through powerful guilds organized under official supervision. Not only was a worker unable to leave his trade for a different occupation, but sons were required to follow their fathers' trades. Artisans actually tried to escape from unprofitable or dangerous occupations, but they were pursued by the police and punished if caught. It was in this way that the government expected to guarantee that production would be kept up, and all productive activity was frankly designed to give preference to food and supplies needed for the army and bureaucracy.

One of the valuable innovations was the reform of the currency and of the mint system introduced by Diocletian. This put an end—though only for a time—to the inflation which the government had favored, at least tacitly, for many years. Diocletian then attempted to legislate price-control, but this proved impossible to enforce.

Antioch by reason of its strategic position in Syria was especially affected by these developments. It became the military headquarters for the defense against the Persian invasions, and so became an imperial field headquarters involving the office and functionaries of the governor of Syria. Because of the vital importance of the eastern provinces, these were given a special reorganization as the Diocese of the Orient, whose chief received an exceptional title of Count of the East. In the other geographical groups of provinces, the prefects who supervised the provincial governors, and were directly responsible to the emperor, had civil powers alone. In the eastern lands, however, because of the constant danger from Persia, special powers were needed, and the Count of the East was given both civil and military jurisdiction. He had his headquarters in Antioch, which thus became the seat of a second major administrative organization. The city was now filled with civil-service officials and with troops who were stationed in the camps all around Antioch, or were passing through the city on their way to the eastern frontier.

Such were the effects of one of the currents which had grown out of the decline of the Empire's physical forces. But there was at the same time another current, bringing a new force into the life of the state and its people. This new source of energy, which had even more far-reaching effects than the reforms of the great emperors, was Christianity, which now emerged as a factor in public life. Growing out of the emancipation of Christianity under Constantine the Great, this new stream of vital force brought about the foundation of the Christian Roman Empire, the phenomenal growth of the church, and the beginning of a new culture and a new educational system. The conversion of Constantine not only transformed the Roman Empire but gave a new direction to the whole history of Europe and of the Slavic states.

Through the reign of Diocletian, Christianity had been a persecuted religion whose adherents, because of their beliefs, were *ipso facto* disloyal citizens of the state, as well as impious enemies of the old religion which had made the empire great. But in spite of persecution the power of Christianity had been growing, and it was beginning to gain a footing in the leading circles of the government. In due time the Emperor Constantine himself was converted. He had visions of the Cross and of Christ, and believed that he had been given the power to defeat his enemies. The Cross— which had been manifested to the Emperor in his vision with the admonition, "In this sign conquer"—became an imperial symbol. The circumstances of Constantine's conversion were not wholly clear in all details, and the sincerity and the motives of his conversion were capable of being questioned by detractors of Christianity. But the conversion was joyfully welcomed by Christians, and its real effects, at least, could not be denied. Christianity now began to receive official approval and support.

The imperial conversion, and the gradual emergence of Christianity as the official religion of the state, raised formidable political problems. It was by no means possible to settle all of these at once. The change in the position of Christianity was so sudden and so unexpected that neither the church nor the Emperor had taken thought for all the questions that would emerge from the transformation of the status of the religion.

More than mere change in personal religion was involved. Christianity, formerly a private matter, now became in many respects a public concern. Paganism in its various aspects— that is, in cults, in philosophy, and in literature—had been not only an affair of private preference and belief but had played a major role in public life; and it was in this same sphere of public life that the new position of Christianity raised political questions.

The pagan Roman Empire, existing by virtue of tradition rather than by a constitution, had built up its political cohesion, and had found sanction for the authority of the emperor, on a basis of public cults which were easily superimposed upon whatever form of personal religion or philosophical belief the individual pagan citizens professed. These official cults were the public worship of the personification of Rome and the deification of the emperor. Formal sacrifice to the sovereign was a token of loyalty to the state, and it was their inability to perform this sacrifice that made the Christians disloyal citizens. The emperor was supposed to rule under the guidance of a tutelary deity, one of the gods of the traditional pantheon, and each sovereign was identified with one of these gods—Jupiter, Apollo, Hercules, or (adopting an Eastern cult) the Unconquered Sun. Thus the ruler was provided with a divine sanction for his power, and the diverse peoples within the empire, with their varied forms of traditional religions, were united in one cult of official worship which served to focus the loyalty of the subjects

44

and thus was one of the best means then available of unifying the state.

Constantine himself, coming to power as a pagan Roman emperor, the heir of all his predecessors, was the *pontifex maximus*, the chief priest of the official cults, and his personal guardian deity was Apollo. When he was converted to Christianity, what was to happen? How could a ruler who was individually a Christian continue to be an emperor who was by definition *pontifex maximus*? As pagan emperor, Constantine was officially supposed to have received messages of advice from Apollo. By definition, the emperor was supposed to have a tutelary deity—but what could there be between Constantine, a child of God, and Apollo? Indeed, what was the political basis of the state to be if the emperor was a Christian and if Christianity were to be a favored, even official, religion?

Here were the elements of a new state and a new culture, but Constantine had to proceed cautiously, for it was evident that the whole population of the empire was not going to be converted to Christianity at once, and many of the court officials and high army officers continued to be pagans. In fact the pagan party at court was for a time very strong.

But if the world, in the Christian belief, was the field for the kingdom of God, there must be a place within this kingdom for the sovereignty of a Roman Emperor who was a Christian. If all things were to become new, the Christian Roman Emperor would inaugurate an empire which would play its own part as an instrument in the realization of the Kingdom. Like its predecessor, this new empire needed both a political and a religious basis. The theory of the new state was formulated by Eusebius, bishop of Caesarea, a learned and devout churchman who was one of Constantine's close advisers in ecclesiastical matters. Eusebius worked out a new statement of the nature of the Christian ruler and the sources of his power, in which ancient pagan theories of kingship—including the traditional doctrine of the Roman emperor's power—were in part taken over into a new concept of Christian monarchy which was to have a long history in the world.

The Christian Roman Emperor was presented as the vice-gerent of God on earth, ruling as the deputy and servant of the Supreme Ruler and under his direct guidance. God selected the Emperor, and his election by earthly procedures was the result of divine provision and intervention. The Emperor's decisions represented the divine will, and it was the responsibility of the Emperor to lead his subjects along the way of true worship and of salvation. The Emperor—in line with the Hellenistic theories of monarchy—was the Savior and Benefactor and Good Shepherd of his people. Thus, if the Emperor had great power, he also had great responsibility. If the Christian theory of his rule resembled in so many respects the traditional pagan concept, the transition in the state was so much the easier.

While the Emperor must continue to be the traditional ruler of his pagan subjects—Constantine kept up some of the pagan forms and official symbolism for some years after his conversion to Christianity—here was the basis for a new Christian state. But there were still problems to be worked out, both political and cultural.

Perhaps the most immediate of these was the question of the relationship of the Emperor and the church. If the Emperor was God's representative and counterpart on earth, what position, functionally, was he to occupy in the administrative—even theological—affairs of the church? Related to this was the problem of what relationship the church was to have with the civil authority. If Christianity was to be the state religion, how far should the civil authority, if force should prove necessary, intervene in the discipline of the church? Neither the state nor the church had anticipated or provided for this question.

But the question was not long in presenting itself and demanding a solution. The tremendous invigoration that had come to the church as a consequence of its emancipation resulted in a stimulation of theological speculation that led to more lively and widespread discussion than the church had previously known. At the same time, new questions of organization, internal discipline, and personnel emerged.

The inevitable consequence was controversy and the rise of heresy, and many observers were saddened to see the church's spiritual life overlaid by such unworthy quarrels —though it could only be admitted that some at least of the contention arose from an honest effort to clarify the church's beliefs.

Some of the controversies took on major proportions, and the Donatist and Arian heresies provoked such disorders that they had to be taken into account by the government if public order was to be maintained. More than this, the Emperor Constantine and his advisers believed that the safety and prosperity of the state and the people depended upon their adherence to orthodox doctrine. If the Emperor was now, according to the new Christian political theory, in effect the controlling power in the church, what was his position to be in the matter of the theological controversies? When the contentions of the Arians made it necessary to convoke a council, the Emperor as by right summoned the Council of Nicaea in A.D. 325 and presided at its sessions; and he used the police powers of the state to enforce the council's decisions. The church, grateful for its emancipation and for the imperial favor, readily accepted Constantine's role, without perhaps thinking too much of the ultimate possibilities of imperial domination.

Thus it became accepted that the Emperor not only could but should take a position—under the guidance of the Holy Spirit—when doctrinal matters were in dispute. As a consequence, it became inevitable that contending parties within the church should seek to win the Emperor and his advisers to their side. It was inevitable, too, that matters of episcopal promotion and jurisdiction—sometimes entailing the control of considerable amounts of property—should come to the notice of court officials if not of the Emperor himself. It is not strange that there emerged a type of worldly "political" bishop who devoted himself more to diplomatic maneuvers at the imperial court than to shepherding his flock in some distant city. There was, moreover, the question of legislation, both as it affected Christians and as it began to reflect Christian ethics. Here Constantine was the pioneer in a series of reforms of the existing laws which in time had a major effect on the law of the Christian world. But in all these matters Constantine saw to it that the church was received into the state; the state as such was not taken into the church. The church came into the state on the state's terms. Whether the church fully realized that this was the effect of Constantine's measures is no longer clear and may not have been clear at the time. If the church did understand the nature of the imperial settlement, it may very well have welcomed it without realizing what all the consequences might be.

These consequences had in due time shown themselves, and the situation of the church in the reign of Theodosius was the result. Constantine's sons and successors had taken opposite sides in the Arian controversy, and Constantius, who became emperor of the eastern part of the empire (A.D. 337–62), was an avowed Arian, willing to institute a veritable persecution of the orthodox. The Arians indeed were attempting to set up an Arian state church dominated by the sovereign.

Many people in Antioch could remember the long course of the Arian dispute. The Christological issue—whether Christ was divine or was a subordinate being, created by God but not of the same divine substance as the Father— developed into a variety of derivative heresies, but orthodoxy, though in peril, was stoutly defended by Athanasius of Alexandria. After an interregnum when the pagan Emperor Julian the Philosopher occupied the throne (A.D. 361– 63), the Arian problem again attached itself to the imperial house. The Emperor Valens (A.D. 364–78) was violently Arian and instituted a persecution of orthodox Christians which only ceased—in part at the behest of the pagan orator Themistius—in A.D. 377.

This was what had grown out of the heritage of Constantine the Great. The Arian controversy was itself dying, for Arianism did not contain the inherent strength which would have been necessary if it was to replace orthodoxy and thus alter the fundamental character of Christianity. When Theodosius, an orthodox and deeply religious man, became emperor (A.D. 379), it was evident that peace could be restored in the church; but the course of the controversy, and the role the sovereigns had played in it, had showed that some of the problems that had arisen in Constantine's reign were still to be settled.

But it was not only in the spheres of politics and theology that there had been problems to be worked out. The emergence of Christianity had likewise raised an intellectual question which potentially might entail almost equally far-reaching changes in the culture of the empire. This involved one of the basic characteristics of Graeco-Roman civilization.

In Greek civilization (in Libanius' own phrase) literature and worship of the gods were twin sisters. One could not attack one, or attempt to do away with it, without affecting the other. Every educated Christian—and especially the Christian who had been converted after coming to years of maturity—knew this; and classical literature was so much a part of pagan philosophy and religion, and his literature meant so much to an educated pagan, that a Christian was unable to separate, in his mind, the literature from the people who possessed it and looked to it for their faith and their perspective on life. It was the task of Christians to convert the pagans; but if the Christians at the same time had to look upon the pagans as essentially hostile to them, the Christians could only feel—even unconsciously—that the pagan literature was connected with this hostility.

Such a feeling had been responsible for the reaction of many of the early Christian teachers against pagan literature as such. There was of course good reason for Christians to disapprove of specific parts of the literature, such as the plays of Aristophanes and some of the accounts of the private lives of the gods and goddesses. No Christian child, studying Greek literature, should be exposed to such reading matter, and no Christian adult would wish to harbor the thoughts they suggested. The vices of the pagans as enumerated in the New Testament, and the proverbial reputation of Corinth as a city of pleasure, had not disappeared from the pagan world of Theodosius' time, and pagan artists continued to produce paintings, statues, and mosaics that were joyful salutes to the pleasures of this world. All of this—art, literature, philosophy, and religion—formed, in the eyes of both pagan and Christian, one organic whole. Thus Christianity had found that it had to attack, and paganism to defend, not just a religious belief but a whole way of life and a whole intellectual and artistic system.

But however plain the issue may have seemed, some Christians had come to believe that it was not possible, or indeed wise, to condemn pagan literature *in toto*. This literature was naturally familiar to educated men who were converted to Christianity as adults. Even more important, it continued to form the core of the educational system when Christianity was already flourishing and expanding. This was a matter that affected every individual, whether pagan or Christian, and beyond the individual, the state itself, for the functioning of the state depended upon the education and training of the men who administered it.

The political and economic reforms of Diocletian and Constantine had not included any change in the educational program, for both in theory and in practice the educational system was regarded as eminently satisfactory. Education continued to be based upon the study of the ancient classical authors. The judgment of the fifth-century Athenians was the absolute criterion of good taste; as Cicero wrote (*Orator,* 25), they would listen to no discourse that was not "pure and well chosen." The speaker who wished to please them "dared not use a word that was unusual or offensive." Thus the student in Libanius' day was still trained to learn to understand and appreciate the writings of the classical authors, and the purpose of education was to enable the young man to write and speak in the style of the great masters of antiquity. No one thought of this as slavish copying. The curriculum exhibited the conviction that the ancient writers and philosophers represented the summit of human achievement, in both thought and expression; and since they could not be surpassed, the best thing to do was to try to understand the secret of their mastery, and to imitate them so far as possible. This was indeed imitation, but it was imitation of an intellectual accomplishment that represented the highest standards of human achievement. Ancient literature was "classical" because it had succeeded in recording a timeless picture of humanity in all its aspects. In the pagan view of life the proper study of mankind was man. Thus the student could best be prepared for life—in the family, in the city, and in the state—by a thorough training in this literature of humanity. The classical authors, seeking to depict the life around them, had produced a series of pictures of what was to be emulated and what was to be avoided, and there were works which could be used at all periods of schooling, from earliest youth to maturity.

The classical writings had another value, their literary style. One of the basic beliefs of the educational tradition was that accuracy and clarity of thought were reflected in the written and spoken expression of the thought. A trained and competent mind would inevitably manifest itself in its manner of expression. Conversely a poor command of language and an inability to convey ideas clearly and elegantly could, it was thought, only betoken a poorly equipped and poorly trained mind. The greatest emphasis was placed upon literary style; but this was done for what were considered the best of reasons.

Basically, of course, the considerations which brought this curriculum into being and then maintained it were utilitarian as well as philosophical. It was on this pedagogical basis that men could best be trained for the law and the civil service, and it was officially recognized that advancement in the higher reaches of the civil service depended upon literary achievement.

Such was the educational system that everyone had to

pass through who intended to follow a career in the professions or in public life. But could a Christian be trained in this literature which was sometimes so emphatically unchristian?

Some of the early Christian thinkers had concluded that the only solution was to turn one's back upon the whole of pagan culture. The Christian must be on his guard against "philosophy" and vain deceit, based on man-made teaching. The lawyer Tertullian's famous question, "What has Athens to do with Jerusalem?" epitomized the reaction of many earnest Christians.

But there was also another answer, less abrupt, which had been worked out slowly by a succession of devout Christian thinkers, beginning with such men as Clement of Rome and Justin Martyr among the Apostolic Fathers. Some of these men, trained in the classics, were secure enough in their faith to be able to read the pagan authors from a Christian point of view. The first extensive effort to take the classical authors into the Christian tradition was made by the eminent theologians Clement of Alexandria and Origen. It was plain to them that there were elements in the best of pagan thought and literature that could be useful in the ethical and intellectual training of Christians, as they had been proven to be useful in the training of pagans. Plato in many ways seemed to approximate some aspects of Christian teaching. He could not, of course, come to the highest of the levels that Christianity had opened to mankind; but he had sought the answers to the problems of the nature of man, the nature of the soul, and the basis of human conduct, which had been answered by Christianity; and if Plato was unable to reach the answers himself, his thought was valuable as an expression of what the human mind could accomplish on the basis of reason alone, without the aid of divine revelation. To the

Christian thinker, it was significant that Plato realized that there was an ultimate being and an element of immortality, and that he could not really grasp this or understand it or locate it. The real quest, Plato knew, was for the source of this immortality, and he knew that he was not in a position to find the answer. Seen under this aspect, Plato's thought could be instructive for Christians, and the writings of other classical authors could be valuable for mental discipline and literary training. It was easy to exclude unsuitable or offensive material. The Christian, properly guided, could surely benefit from what was after all one of the noblest elements in his national heritage. Any Christian who studied it sympathetically could perceive that pagan thought at its best contained, within its natural limitations, a universal element which fitted into the larger universality of Christianity. Christian thought would be enriched, not altered, if the best elements of pagan experience were subsumed in it.

It was just before Theodosius came to the throne that the right of Christians to study and profit from the pagan classics had been vindicated in definitive fashion by the work of the three great Cappadocian theologians, Basil of Caesarea, his younger brother Gregory of Nyssa, and their friend and co-worker Gregory of Nazianzen. These thinkers had perceived that the new position of Christianity and its new responsibilities and privileges made it all the more necessary to put Christianity in a position in which it could enjoy its true heritage and work out the new Christian culture which was obviously needed if Christianity was to fulfill its mission and replace completely the pagan world. And until this consummation could be achieved, Christians and pagans still had to live in one world, and Christians would have to share with the pagans such aspects of this world as could not be altered immediately.

Thus it was that in the days of the most Christian Emperor Theodosius the humanistic culture of the new Christian empire was coming into its full heritage. Christians could now recognize that true faith could be both strong enough and wide enough to admit the intellectual heritage of ancient Greece in its best aspects, and transform it for Christian use. Thus the mundane culture of the Christian world could find its proper place as an adjunct to the religious teaching. Now the intellectual, religious, and political aspects of man's life could be integrated into one harmonious whole within the divine sanction and under the authority of the divine dispensation. The hostility on the cultural level between paganism and Christianity had grown out of conflicting ideas concerning the source of human knowledge and the authority which this source represented. Pagans and Christians each claimed to possess the truth. While some pagans might recognize the existence of an Unknown God, most pagan writers and thinkers had conceived of man and his reasoning powers as the center of creative effort. It was possible for man to set out to discover the truth; and while there had been imagined a whole series of gods and of diverse divine forces which might aid man in his effort, it was still possible for man to discover the ultimate meaning of things. To the Greek mind, knowledge was unlimited, and the trained human intellect had before it an unbounded field of inquiry and speculation. The Christian apologists pointed out that the existence of such a variety of deities imagined by the Greeks, and the existence of such a variety of their philosophical systems, cast doubt on the validity of all their beliefs. Still, to the pagan, it was the human mind which was capable of setting out to discover the truth, of judging the results, and of continuing the search if it was supposed that something more was to be found.

In contrast, Christians could be certain that their knowledge and their wisdom came from the same authority that guaranteed the truth of their faith. Along with understanding, they had been given the ability to distinguish between good and evil. The whole Christian system formed one truth, represented in Christ. On this basis the church and the Christian people could with confidence create and enjoy and profit from a true Greek Christian culture, and so it was that forty years after the death of Constantine the Great the world of the Christian empire was beginning to emerge in the true shape toward which the conversion of Constantine had begun to guide it. The process had had to be a gradual one, and the conversion of the Graeco-Roman world was not even yet complete; but the Christians of Theodosius' day could perhaps feel more confident and more content than their fathers and grandfathers had under Constantine the Great. Thus at Antioch, long both a distinguished home of Greek culture and an influential center of Christian life, the reign of Theodosius marked a new stage in the maturing of the Christian state. The process was at work of course throughout the Graeco-Roman world. In Antioch the development was the more consequential because of the strength there of the two strands, pagan and Christian, which were being brought together.

But the process was necessarily a long one, and what was achieved under Theodosius was not final. The ultimate development, in both culture and politics, had to wait for the reign of Justinian the Great in the sixth century. Yet the foundations of Justinian's work went back to Constantine and Theodosius. What was being worked out was a unity of religion, politics, and intellectual culture which was to give the East Roman and Byzantine Empire its peculiar stamp.

It was in Antioch as a city, both Greek polis and Christian community, that such cultural fusion took place. It was in the city, the human community, that teaching, study, creative effort, and social interchange made possible both the maintenance of an old civilization and the formation of a new one, just as an old religion survived, or a new one spread, only in a human community. In this process as it was worked out in the fourth century all the great cities—Antioch, Constantinople, Alexandria, Athens—had a part to play. The result—in Theodosius' time and later—represented the combined action of the particular traditions of all these cities. Within the city, of course, it was the citizen who acted and contributed to determining the result; but it was still the city that shaped the citizen.

CHAPTER IV

THE GOOD FORTUNE OF ANTIOCH

"It is men that make a city."

—THUCYDIDES

IN the time of Theodosius the Great, Antioch was one of the famous centers of education in the Greek-speaking world. In part of course this was due to the work of Libanius, but Libanius was the pupil and successor of older generations of teachers whose fame had brought students to Antioch from all over the world. There is no doubt that many of his fellow citizens would have agreed with Libanius' attempt to sum up the reasons for the greatness of Antioch:

What city can we say is worthy to be compared with this? More fortunate than the oldest, it is superior to some in size, surpasses others in the nobility of its lineage, and others in its all-producing territory. By one (Constantinople) it may be excelled in walls, but it is greater than this in the abundance of its water and in the mildness of its winter, in the refinement of its inhabitants and in its pursuit of learning; and it is more fair than that city which is even larger (Rome), because of that fairest thing, Hellenic education and literature.

In the Roman Empire of that day, education was recognized as being one of the essential bases for both the welfare of the state and the happiness of its citizens. A competent training in the humanities was officially recognized as a prerequisite for entry into the government service, and evi-

dence of distinction in learning and literary skill—as shown
for example by publication of works on history or philosophy, or by poems in the classical style—earned advancement
in the civil service. The emperors themselves often had
literary aspirations— the Emperor Julian had been a learned
philosopher and man of letters of real gifts, and would have
been a distinguished figure by his own right in the history
of Greek literature and philosophy—and at least in principle
they were supposed to seek the advice of professional philosophers in affairs of state. Themistius and others were appointed ambassadors to foreign states because of their learning and literary accomplishments. Among the Christians,
bishops were not infrequently scholars with large personal
libraries, familiar with pagan learning as well as with scrip-
ture and theology, and priests knew that their success as
preachers and apologists would be enhanced if their sermons
were composed and delivered according to the rules of rhetoric of the traditional classical course of study.

Yet the organization and support of the educational system was largely a private affair, rather than a responsibility
and a public service of the government. The municipalities
on occasion called public professors of rhetoric and literature, and paid their stipends (a distinguished man of letters
might find himself the happy recipient of simultaneous in-
vitations from competing municipalities), and the imperial
administration supported a university with a library in Constantinople, paying the salaries of the professors; but beyond
this the state did very little, and in the earlier years of schooling the education a child received depended entirely upon
the financial means of the parents and upon what kind of
private instruction happened to be available locally.

The economic conditions of the time being what they were
—the Roman Empire had always exhibited a contrast be-

tween extremes of wealth and poverty, with a relatively small "middle class"—it is not surprising that there was a high degree of illiteracy. Ancient thinkers—Aristotle a typical example among them—believed that men were not born equal, but that some possessed greater natural endowments than others, so that some were born to rule, others to serve. In such a concept of humanity, slavery was a natural condition. A man of humble or servile birth, it was believed, was not suited for education, for the difficult, if not degrading, physical surroundings in which he lived could only warp and twist his mind and render it incapable of acquiring or using knowledge. This being the case, it was clearly against nature to try to educate the lower classes or slaves.

If illiteracy was accepted as part of the natural order of things, those responsible for the state never seem to have realized that illiteracy, and indeed lack of education in general, might become a political problem. The Roman Empire, growing gradually as it did, had come to be composed of a polyglot group of nations representing quite different ethnic backgrounds, which needed some common bond by means of which they could be held together. An effort had been made to provide such a bond by developing the official cult of the emperor, which was not so much religious worship as a declaration of loyalty (it was for their refusal to take part in this worship that Christians were regarded as disloyal and persecuted). This, however, was not really sufficient to bind together all the diversified people of the empire. In time of course Christianity would serve as a cohesive factor, but by the end of the fourth century it had not yet reached a sufficient proportion of the population to be a leading force in national unity, as it later became in the Byzantine state.

There was still one factor that might have been developed

as a source of unity, as it was in later times and other places, namely education and culture. A system of free public education promoting the spread of the Greek language in the eastern part of the empire, and along with the language a consciousness of a national heritage of Greek classical culture, ought to have provided a common ground which would have brought together the varied indigenous peoples in Anatolia, Syria, Palestine, and Egypt who otherwise could have felt no common interest. Of course many of these people learned Greek for business purposes, or in order to advance themselves by serving in the government; but their less enterprising or less fortunate brothers, knowing no language save their native tongue, could only feel themselves the subjects of a ruling power of alien language and culture.

The political dangers of this situation, with the possibilities of nationalistic aspirations and even separatism, seem never to have come home to the imperial authorities. Not very long after Theodosius' reign it became all too clear what might be accomplished by political and religious demagogues, appealing to the local patriotism of illiterate Syrian and Egyptian peasants, including illiterate monks. But this again, apparently, was accepted as part of the natural order of things, and when the time came, the central government tried to repress such dangerous movements by force. In the meantime, the existence in Theodosius' day, in Antioch and in the country round about it, of a lower class of farmers and laborers who spoke only Syriac continued as a reminder, to which no one paid very much attention, that there was in fact a separate element in the population that no one tried officially and systematically to integrate with the dominant Greek culture and society. There are indeed records of individuals, bearing indigenous Semitic names, who were able by luck and ability to raise themselves to find acceptance and success in the Greek-speaking level of the local world, but these were the exceptions rather than the rule.

So it was that there were two kinds of children in Antioch: those who could hope to receive an education and those who could not. For the former, learning began usually at home. The child was taught to read and form letters, often by a grandmother, sometimes by an older brother or sister, or in some families by an educated slave. We hear of farmers who spent the winter months, when the weather kept them from working outdoors, carving the letters of the alphabet out of blocks of wood.

At the age of about seven, children would begin to go to school. A child was chaperoned by a family servant or slave, the "pedagogue," who carried the child's books and writing materials to and from school and also acted generally as the child's friend and instructor in manners and morals. The pedagogue was in effect a member of the family and could be a person of great influence, along with the parents.

The schoolmaster never seems to have advanced beyond a humble, almost despised status. He was badly paid, and often ill-tempered, and some children had to suffer severely from tyranny and excessive physical punishment. One reason for the low condition of the calling was that it was not considered necessary for the elementary schoolmaster to possess any special qualifications for his work. There was no licensing of teachers, and no public inspection of schools.

The child would begin by studying elementary grammar and literary composition, and by reading aloud and memorizing stories and passages of "good literature," using anthologies designed for the purpose. Arithmetic was taught much later than it is in modern times. Among the classical authors,

Homer was pre-eminent, as the universal writer in whose works could be found a complete description of humanity in all its aspects. From Homer the child could be taught the basis of morality and the varieties of human character, as well as the appreciation of great literature. Thus the reading of Homer appeared very early in the course of study, and remained there through the higher grades.

What would now be called secondary education began at about the age of twelve. It was not financially possible for all children to reach this stage, for it was sometimes necessary for them to go to work before this age to help support the family.

The child could by this time read and write easily, and was able to begin the serious part of education, which was the detailed study of the classical writers. Both prose writers and poets were taken as models, and the child was taught to imitate their style and to declaim from memory both passages from the authors and original compositions in the same style by the student. That phrases and style might come readily, the student learned extended passages by heart; all through the process of education, indeed, memory was regarded as a more certain way of storing knowledge than by entrusting it to notes or books.

Every detail of literary art was closely studied. Voice, gestures, and posture of the speaker were carefully trained according to established rules, for in later life the success of a public speaker would depend upon appearance and deportment as well as upon the substance of his discourse.

In the study of the authors, the child was introduced to the principles of literary criticism and to scientific philology and grammar. Thus the student learned to analyze and explain a text in its literary, moral, and technical aspects. Of these, the moral content was the chief end of study, for the goal of all education was the formation of character and preparation for life.

The course of study was primarily literary, but mathematics, music, and astronomy were included. Mathematics was studied not so much for practical use as for intellectual discipline which purified the mind and prepared it for the study of philosophy, which was regarded as the highest of all the academic subjects.

This type of training continued until an age which varied between fifteen and twenty, depending upon the student's personal circumstances. At this point, there would come a decisive break in the student's educational career. Some, of course, had to stop here. Those who could continue now embarked upon what were considered higher studies, corresponding to a university course.

This advanced training might continue for several years or more, depending again on the student's financial resources and upon his interests and future plans. Some indeed continued their advanced studies for as much as eight years.

Almost always at this stage, the young man would go abroad, to such places as Athens or Constantinople, seeking to study with a particular teacher whose fame had attracted him. The personal relationship between teacher and pupil, important at every stage of ancient education, now took on a decisive significance, for classical culture was a culture of the person. Learning, taste, manners, and morals were all transmitted in personal association between master and pupil; and there was a very strong sense of the handing on of a great tradition in the higher stages of the educational process. Eminent men of letters, and others who achieved intellectual distinction, all looked back upon a beloved teacher whose influence had been decisive in shaping their careers.

Under his chosen master—in some cases under a succession of masters, as the student might go to different professors in one place, such as Athens, or might travel from city to city—the young man would embark on the study of the finer points of rhetoric, composition, and literary history and criticism, as well as the history of philosophy. The art of composition and delivery was taught by the study of a variety of literary forms, such as fictitious speeches of great characters of history, debates, descriptions of works of art, forensic speeches, literary essays on topics of general interest, descriptions of episodes of mythology. The training was designed to develop literary taste, skill, and originality. Young men who intended to follow the law or a public career were prepared to appear before critical audiences of their elders who had all gone through the same training. For a lawyer, literary style, the manner of delivery, and the personal impression made by the speaker were almost as important as actual knowledge of the law, which was studied only after the training in public speaking had been acquired.

His education completed, the young man had to choose his career. This was often of course settled for him by family interests. If it was to be the teaching of rhetoric and literature, he was by this point considered to be sufficiently prepared, and he could set himself up as a teacher wherever he could find a suitable opportunity.

For a young man of ambition with the necessary ability—and if possible with useful family connections—the most promising career might be the law. Private practice could be lucrative and might lead to a social position of great prestige.

The training of lawyers being a matter of such vital concern to the government, private instruction, once permitted, was no longer sanctioned, and the law student could only attend the schools maintained by the government at Constantinople and at Berytus (Beirut). The course lasted five years. The professor read and explained the texts and the classic commentaries of the celebrated lawyers of the earlier empire. This meant the *Institutes* of Gaius, and Ulpian, for the first-year men, more Ulpian in the second year, Papinian in the third year, Paulus in the fourth. The fifth year was devoted to the imperial constitutions or decisions which had been collected at the end of the third century.

The student used two collections of laws, the Gregorian Code and the Hermogenian Code, which had been edited on private initiative; it was not until the reign of Theodosius the Younger, fifty years later, that the government issued an official code of laws.

Most of the students in the eastern lands of the empire spoke Greek, but instruction in the law schools was in Latin, the language of the laws themselves, though there was some effort in the time of Theodosius the Great to introduce Greek. Libanius and other conservative teachers in Antioch were distressed because the young men of the city devoted time to the study of Latin and of shorthand—an asset for legal work—which (their teachers thought) they ought to have devoted to the traditional literary studies.

Training in the law was essential for a career in the imperial civil service. This career was attractive not only because of the social prestige it carried but because the higher posts could make their occupants wealthy, as well as giving them patronage of appointments. It was, however, not always easy to find an opening, and a qualified applicant might have to wait before he could secure an appointment. A civil servant's income depended partly upon his salary, partly upon the fees which by custom he was allowed to collect from the members of the public who had to have dealings with him. The fees being an attractive aspect of the work, there was great competition for places, and the various civil-service offices had to have fixed tables of organization, lest they expand beyond due measure. Thus it was much better for a young man, if he hoped to follow this career, to have a personal connection which would start him on the hierarchical ladder.

The young man who wished to follow one of the technical professions, such as medicine, architecture, or engineering, did not enjoy the same facilities for study as the aspirant in rhetoric or law. A knowledge of mathematics and the physical sciences, so far as they were then developed, was always considered to be an essential part of the liberal education, but the traditional view still prevailed—now somewhat anachronistically—that a gentleman did not soil his hands by pursuing a technical career. Hence knowledge of such subjects as medicine and architecture was divided into two categories, the "theoretical" and the "practical." The gentleman learned the former; the latter was supposed to be left for persons of lesser education. However, the attraction of this kind of work was for some individuals so strong that young men of good family did become physicians and architects, though there were times during the fourth century when there were not enough candidates to supply all the practitioners needed. The training, indeed, was sometimes difficult to find, and it varied in quality, for there were no official and recognized professors of these subjects, and a young man had to find a practitioner who was willing to take apprentices. The apprentice might in time become a full-fledged assistant. A good teacher, interested in his young men, could do much to advance his profession; but there were no licenses or government examinations, and it is not surprising that poorly trained men sometimes set themselves up in practice.

The army and the church always attracted a certain number of aspirants. A young man who wished to follow a military career, and was of officer material, was trained as a cadet—in Constantinople, if he were fortunate—and began to serve as a junior officer at an early age. Training for the Christian ministry depended upon a counterpart of the apprentice system—study under a priest or a bishop—which will be described in a later chapter.

The young man, whether he was following a profession or (in the case of the leading families) devoting himself to the care of the family property, found himself faced with the varied responsibilities which had come to be a part of citizenship in a city such as Antioch in the days of Theodosius the Great.

By the time of Theodosius, the machinery of municipal administration reflected a development arising from conditions on account of which the central imperial government had found it necessary to turn over to local magistrates and city councils (called by the traditional title of senates) both the maintenance of municipal public services and the collection of imperial taxes. In a city such as Antioch, the imperial government in Constantinople was represented by a number of officials concerned with provincial administration, higher legal jurisdiction, and the military establishment, all of them members of the intricately organized and rigidly controlled civil-service system. Such were the Count of the East, the Master of the Soldiers, and the governor of Syria, all with their appropriate staffs. But the officials responsible for the daily life of the city—for the maintenance of streets and sewers; the heating of the public baths; the public entertainments, including the Olympic Games; the inspection and regulation of public markets to ensure fair weights and other commercial standards; inspection of the public water supply (people had to be kept from washing clothes in public fountains which were supposed to supply drinking water); provision for street lighting, which had to be furnished by owners of shops, who were required to place lights before their doors at night; provision for the supply of bread, the staple food, which had to be assured, and at fixed prices—the men responsible for all these services were members of the local senatorial class who, if of proper ancestry, possessing property representing a certain value, were obliged to contribute both their personal services and their money to the maintenance of these public functions.

In addition the members of the senatorial order were obliged, by their property qualification and their inherited status, to perform certain local services for the imperial government, services which were, indeed, of vital nature, such as the collection of imperial taxes, the requisitioning of animals from private owners for the use of the army and the imperial postal system; the requisitioning of the supplies of food and materials for the army; the raising of recruits for the army and the requisitioning of the labor of farmers and others for road-building and other public works such as the maintenance of bridges and of the fortification walls of Antioch.

As the authoritarian state developed, it had come to be believed that this was the only way in which the municipalities could be kept going; but the system inevitably entailed many hardships and many abuses. Collection of the ordinary taxes, for example, was difficult enough, but if an extraordinary tax was imposed, as was done from time to time to raise money for special purposes or to cover an unusual deficit, then the senator responsible for its collection was faced not only with the personal difficulty and even personal risk involved in extracting the money but with the possibility that, if he failed to produce the required sum, he might be held personally responsible for it. The government, in instituting this system of collection, had made sure that it would receive the money from someone.

One of the most onerous, and also most important, of the duties was the provision of horses for the horse and chariot races which were one of the most popular public entertainments at Antioch, and the supplying of wild animals for the animal fights and hunts in the amphitheatre on the mountainside which were another intensely popular amusement, having succeeded the gladiatorial combats which had disappeared when Christianity became the state religion. The public of Antioch possessed a highly developed taste in these matters, and insisted on the best in horses and wild beasts, and the supply of both was no longer so plentiful that it was easy to meet the requirements of a city as devoted to its pleasures as Antioch. When the mountains east and north of Antioch had been fully exploited—Antioch was not the only city looking for entertainment for its people—it was necessary sometimes to go some distance for lions and bears and the smaller animals, and it was not uncommon to have to send to Spain for horses. Sometimes indeed the senator upon whom this duty fell had to travel extensively—and of course at his own expense—searching for animals. The citizen who presented the games became an object of great public adulation, but this was also one of the most expensive of the public services.

But the greatest hazard of the system was the possible effect upon the family property of the senator whose means did not really allow him to meet the expenses of the service he was compelled to perform. Originally the necessity of performing these services had been looked upon as an opportunity for a public-spirited citizen to show his generosity and his devotion to his fellow citizens and to the honor of their municipality, and he was rewarded by his place in the public eye, by personal prestige, and sometimes by a statue or bust of himself, with an honorific inscription, erected by the grateful people of the city. But the inevitable happened. Some citizens whose birth and property should have rendered them liable to the performance of public services preferred not to spend their substance in this way, and by various means—including personal influence and bribery—they were able to evade their responsibilities. Some occupations, such as the imperial civil service, the Christian ministry, and the teaching profession, were granted immunity from taxes and public services. Immunity was sometimes granted to encourage recruitment in a profession, such as medicine, architecture, and engineering, in which there was a shortage of man power. Sometimes senators who found their situation intolerable simply fled the city.

The result of exemption, evasion, and flight could only be added burdens for those senators who were unable to escape the duties of their station, and a senator might easily find himself impoverished by the demands which were imposed upon him. Some senators even remained unmarried because they did not wish to have their children suffer the hardships which they themselves had undergone.

At the same time there were many men, not of senatorial family, whose success in business or as landowners had brought them substantial fortunes, who were able by illicit means to avoid being taken into the senatorial classes in which their new property qualification should have placed them. It was remembered that the Emperor Julian, finding the whole municipal government of Antioch in a disorganized and inefficient condition, had forcibly enlarged the senate by compelling such men to serve in it, but reforms of this kind sometimes did not last very long.

One of the most difficult, as also one of the most important, problems was the maintenance of the food supply. Here Antioch was more fortunate than many cities, for the region all about it was fertile and well watered, and in normal times produced an adequate and varied supply of cereal crops (especially wheat and barley), fruit (it was both eaten fresh and preserved by drying in the sun), and vegetables; and the glory of Antioch was its abundance of seafood, taken from the Mediterranean, the Orontes River, and the Lake of Antioch. Libanius in his encomium of the city wrote proudly of the hospitality Antioch could offer:

> Thus travelers who have drawn near the city when it has grown dark in the last stage of their journey push on to the city in good spirits, since they know they will fare well here even at night. It is possible for them both to bathe and to dine more magnificently than men invited to feasts of victory after public games, just as if the cooks had been sent ahead to make preparations. Everything is at once available, and it is not necessary to hurry about in search of fish, but only to listen for the peddlers in the streets as they shout. Indeed, we who live on land enjoy more fish than many of those who are tossed about on the ocean, and although we are separated from the sea, the fishermen catch for us in their nets the creatures of the sea, and crowds of fishes of all kinds come into them every day. Another fine thing here is that the needy are not deprived of this kind of food. Fortune, who has distributed fitting things to each man, has given to the wealthy the products of the sea, to others those of the lake, and to both in common has given

the river, which nourishes for the wealthy the kind of fish which comes up to it from the sea, and for the others the other kinds, all of them in abundance.

In normal times, then, Antioch was well off for food. But there were major dangers to which ancient farming and the contemporary economy were peculiarly exposed. Growing crops could be damaged or destroyed by insects or by plant diseases, against which there was no known remedy. There were periodic visitations of locusts, and plagues recurred among cattle, again with no known remedy. Farmers and landowners had to accept all these hazards as part of the established order.

But in a region with a climate such as that of Syria, the greatest danger came from the changes of the weather. The continued success of the crops, season after season, depended in the end upon the regularity of the water supply, and nature would not guarantee this. The summer was hot and without rain, and nothing could be grown during that season except in gardens which could be watered by human labor from storage reservoirs or springs. The regular growing season for farm crops was the rainy winter, and crops sown in the autumn were harvested in the spring. This meant that if there were a drought during the winter the whole spring crop would be lost.

This in fact is what happened, and not too infrequently. The result would be immediate and growing hardship for the lower classes. Prosperous farmers and landowners possessed stores of food and could feed themselves. They would, of course, hold their stocks and refuse to sell them until prices had begun to go up; shopkeepers would do the same. The government would do what it could to import food, but land transport was so cumbersome and slow that the cost was prohibitive, and it was not always possible to obtain relief from the grain-growing lands of Egypt and North Africa whose production was wholly consumed by the areas they normally supplied, notably the great cities, Rome and Constantinople, which were wholly incapable of feeding themselves.

All this meant, of course, that as the scarcity of food continued, prices advanced, and in time the situation might become so serious, especially for the poor, that there were often riots. In a severe famine, the farmers themselves might be forced to come into the city seeking relief. If a certain amount of publicly owned wheat and barley was on hand (barley bread was eaten by the poor; wheaten bread by the well-to-do) or if it had been possible to import some grain, a limited supply of bread would be available, but this would have to be baked and distributed under the strictest supervision. Guards would be posted at the city gates to prevent farmers and travelers from carrying out more than their share of bread. When things came to such a crisis, the bakers would try to flee from the city, for they knew that they might be blamed by the people or the authorities, or both.

Some governors of Syria, in such a juncture, would issue price-control decrees. The effect would be that all food would immediately disappear from the market. The landowners and shopkeepers knew that the decrees could not be enforced and that if they held their stocks long enough, they could sell them at higher prices. Some merchants simply went out of business when price control was imposed. The senators and municipal authorities, who should have felt their responsibility for maintaining whatever food supply was available, often engaged in speculation themselves, and if they were landowners or businessmen they looked first to their own interests and those of their friends. Many people at Antioch in Theodosius' time could remember the great famine under the

Emperor Julian, twenty years before, which, as one looked back on it, was certainly one of the factors that contributed to the failure of Julian's whole religious and political program, for his efforts to deal with the shortage of food—caused by a drought which ruined crops—simply turned all classes in Antioch, rich and poor, against him. Landowners and senators had protested against his price control because, they said, famines were a part of the natural order of things and were to be endured; prices would regulate themselves, and come down eventually. Such indeed was the natural reaction of the ruling class of those days. Every time a famine was caused by a drought, the shortage of food could have been predicted at least a few months ahead, for the meaning of lack of rain during the growing season was unmistakable; yet we never hear of any advance public preparation to deal with a coming famine.

Such were some of the internal problems that the citizens of Antioch had to face. Other problems arose from local relationships with some of the imperial officials whose duties brought them to the city. Antioch did indeed enjoy unusual advantages, commercially and socially, in being the capital of the province of Syria and seat of the administration of the Diocese of the East, as well as headquarters for the armies defending the Mesopotamian frontier. These advantages, however, were sometimes offset by the troubles the citizens experienced with the officials who represented the central government.

Some such troubles, at least, were almost inevitable, since the governors, and sometimes even the Counts of the East, were often appointed not because of merit or ability but because they were favorites of some high official in the imperial administration. When they arrived at Antioch, they might let it be known quite openly that their chief interest during their tenure of office would be to enrich themselves in whatever way they could. Personal profit was in fact one of the recognized perquisites of the provincial administrator, who was expected to take advantage of his position in order to supplement his salary. It was true that a well-disposed administrator would repay his capital city to a certain extent by presenting it with a public building, such as a portico, as a souvenir of his sojourn, but this would not wholly take away the bad taste left by what amounted to legalized extortion.

Naturally there were some people in Antioch ready to assist the governor in any way he desired, hoping to make something for themselves in the process. This meant that if a governor arrived who had any personal inclination to profligate company, it would not be long before he was surrounded by a group which could, by catering to his enjoyments, have a major part in shaping his administration.

There was another important respect in which a governor's personal character was a matter of vital concern for the people of Antioch. In addition to being responsible for the functioning of the province, the governor served as a judge, both trying certain types of cases involving the affairs of the province, including the city of Antioch, and hearing appeals from the decisions of lower judges who sat in Antioch and elsewhere in the province. The amount of legal training and experience a judge might possess could vary considerably. Moreover, the governor as judge had absolute control over the conduct of the trials. In those days when a witness was as a matter of course flogged during his examination in order to make sure that his testimony would be correct, and when it was considered necessary to torture the accused in order to make him tell the truth, a governor of Syria who happened to possess a streak of cruelty could cause much unhappiness in the city. Some governors were so cruel that complaints were made to the emperor, and they were removed from office. But of course not all officials were cruel and rapacious. Some at least were upright and benevolent men, and we hear of their benefactions to the city.

Antioch had been an important military center from its earliest days. Under Theodosius it was no longer the headquarters and staging area for annual campaigns against the Persians, as it had been under Constantius and Julian; but the defense of the Persian frontier was still a major requirement for the stability and safety of the empire. There were camps and and training grounds everywhere in the neighborhood, especially on the level plain across the Orontes, and the city was filled with the officers and clerks of the staff of the general in command, as well as with the soldiers who were allowed to come in to the city when off duty. The presence of such numbers of soldiers had a marked effect on the city's economy and tended to keep prices high. Libanius gives us a vivid picture of what the city would be like when a major campaign was being prepared:

> When this last Persian war was unchained, for which the Persian government had been preparing for a long time, and when the emergency called for adequate counter-preparation to match the threat, and even more than preparations, called for a place capable of receiving all those things that such a war requires, this land of ours is the one that rose above the emergency with its abundance and collected the forces to its bosom and sent forth the entire army, when the time called. For there flowed into it, like rivers to the sea, all the soldiers, all the bowmen and horsemen and the horses, both those of the fighting men and those carrying burdens, and every camel and every band of soldiers, so that the ground was covered with men standing and men sitting; the walls were covered with shields hung up and spears and helmets were to be seen

77

everywhere; everything resounded with hammering and noise and whinnying, and there were so many units stationed here that their officers alone would have added no small population to the city. Such a great army was gathered that in other places the drinking water would have been exhausted; but everyone received the soldiers as pleasantly as though they were caring for a kinsman who came for a visit after a long interval; and each one fared as well from the land as though each house in the city had been turned into a storehouse filled with provisions. The men could in this way be nourished to satiety, so that it seemed that it was not human intention or labor which provided the foresight or the service, but as though the gods, as the power of gods is, prepared everything in unseen fashion . . . . We provide this city as a base of operations which rivals the warlike prowess of the emperor, and we do not dampen his eager courage by any defect in our help.

Antioch had in fact been the home of the distinguished military officer Ammianus Marcellinus, who, after an active career, turned historian. As a result of his career—and this was very unusual for a native of Antioch—he settled in Rome, early in the reign of Theodosius, and there wrote his history in Latin.

Behind the officials, the bureaucrats, and the soldiers, behind the visiting dignitaries, brought into the city by the imperial post, in fact behind all the varied aspects of life in the city, stood the figure of the emperor. It would take a special messenger a week, traveling at top speed and making use of all the facilities of the imperial postal system with its relays of horses and carriages, to go from Antioch to the imperial court at Constantinople; yet the figure of the sovereign was a very real presence, making itself felt in all the operations of the government.

As the empire had developed, especially in the last hundred years before Theodosius' reign, the personal character of the ruler played a more and more important part in all phases of the empire's life. The emperor it was true was not an irresponsible autocrat, for he was subject to some checks, and of course the possibility of revolution always existed. Still the amount of power and of initiative which centered in the sovereign, along with the prestige of his office and his personal influence through his choice of advisers and top officials, meant that the whole existence of the state took its tone from the personality—and in this century the religion as well —of the man who had been fortunate enough to make himself emperor. The principle of heredity was maintained at least in theory, and the system by which a sovereign appointed and adopted a younger colleague, who would in principle succeed him, gave what stability and continuity was possible in the system.

The emperor as an individual possessed power—and responsibility—which was delegated to all his officials throughout the realm. Every functionary, from the great cabinet ministers in Constantinople down through the hierarchy to the lowest clerk in a tax office in a village on the edge of the desert in Egypt, was the personal representative of the emperor and acted and spoke in his name. Judges sat beneath a portrait of the emperor and pronounced their sentences in his name—as extensions, so to speak, of his personal power. Oaths were taken before a painting or statue of the sovereign.

If the emperor was endowed by virtue of his office with a set of official characteristics and powers, as father of his people, there might still be a question whether his personal history and his human personality corresponded to the needs and responsibilities of his office. Men in Antioch who had reached their middle years by the time Theodosius came to the throne could remember four, perhaps even five, emperors (Libanius, born in A.D. 314, could remember six); and it was

79

easy to recall the ways in which life in the city had been affected as these rulers, all different from one another, came to the throne in succession. Theodosius' reign indeed in some ways promised an era of peace; but the citizen of Antioch was prepared by history and by personal experience to accept, so far as he could, whatever a new reign brought.

Constantius, last son of Constantine the Great to reign (A.D. 337–61), vigorous and capable ruler, vehement supporter of the Arian heresy, had been succeeded by his cousin Julian, last member of the Constantinian house, Christian by birth who had turned pagan, courageous general and skillful administrator, at the same time man of letters, philosopher, mystic, and learned historian of religion. His reign of twenty months (A.D. 361–63), largely spent in Antioch, had allowed him to try to re-establish the old religion and do away with Christianity. The effort had failed, but there had been such a crisis that his successor Jovian, a Christian army officer, had had to proclaim an official policy of toleration. Jovian's reign of only eight months (A.D. 363–64) had chiefly been marked by the conclusion of an "ignoble peace" with Persia, as also by an effort—unsuccessful—to bring peace to the church where the Arian dispute was still raging.

After Jovian's sudden death (from overeating, or from the fumes of a stove, according to different accounts) the empire had been ruled by Valentinian (A.D. 364–75), another Christian army officer, and his younger brother Valens. Valentinian, taking the western half of the empire, was tolerant in the religious controversies, but he had a furious temper which dominated all his actions and colored his whole reputation as a ruler.

It was Valens who was remembered in Antioch as the immediate predecessor (A.D. 364–78) of Theodosius as ruler of the East. It was Theodosius' good fortune, in Antioch at least, that he succeeded a man whom few regretted. Valens had in fact spent a good part of his reign at Antioch, and although he had presented the city with the fine new forum known by his name, his memory was particularly execrated in the city. Valens' good qualities, his personal temperance and his consideration for the people of the provinces, were outweighed by his abnormal cruelty and by his permitting himself to be guided by unworthy favorites. He was a coward, in reality unfit to be a ruler, and as a militant Arian he had instituted a veritable persecution of the orthodox Christians. His death in the calamitous battle of Adrianople against the Goths was a deliverance for the people of the empire.

This was the situation into which Theodosius (A.D. 379–95) came. A Spaniard, son of a distinguished army officer and governor of Britain, Theodosius had himself had a noteworthy career as an army officer and provincial governor. A serious and deeply religious man, he was devoted to the service of the empire and of the church. Immediately on his accession he began to work for the peace of the church and the restoration of unity, for the problem was political as well as religious and the division within the church threatened the stability of the whole of society and of the state. At the same time the Emperor initiated new and more severe measures for the suppression of paganism.

In this century of change and transition, it was difficult for life within the empire to be peaceful and prosperous for all citizens at all times. Peace and prosperity in fact might in some ways seem to be almost relative conceptions. But by comparison with the years immediately preceding it, Theodosius' reign had brought improvement in some respects. It was the disaster at Adrianople that had ended Valens' career; but the army was being rebuilt. Peace in the church had brought a tranquillity where before there had been discord.

For the time being, at least, there was no war with Persia. The Emperor was a respected figure, even if his policy was hardly welcome to pagans; but it was possible for pagans such as Themistius to hold high office under him. Antioch could feel that at least it need not look forward to a reign of terror such as Valens had set on foot when he discovered that certain persons—among them, indeed, Libanius—were endeavoring through magical means to discover the name of his successor.

While political and religious developments throughout the empire, and local troubles and problems in Antioch, seemed to occupy the outward life of the citizens, there was another current of life, social and intellectual, which was still not vitally affected by public events. It was in fact a very old current, such as could be displaced only by a major up-heaval. It represented indeed the Greek tradition. Plato had put into words in the *Phaedrus* the Greek love of human association and intellectual occupation: "Everyone knows that one must converse with somebody, either because of friendship or because it is pleasant for some other reason." This was one of the pleasures of life in Antioch as Libanius saw it. Indeed the climate itself favored social and intellectual intercourse by allowing easy association even during the winter. Libanius' encomium gives us a vivid picture of life in Antioch during the winter months:

> It seems to me that one of the most pleasing things in cities, and one of the most useful, is meetings and mixings with other people. That is indeed a city, where there is much of this. Truly, it is good to speak, and to hear is better and to converse is best, and to add what is fitting to the fortunes of one's friends, rejoicing with them in some things, sorrowing with them in others, and to have the same return from them; and in addition to these there are ten thousand things in being

near to one another. People in other cities who do not have stoas along the streets before their houses are scattered by the winter; and although they can be said to live in one city, they are actually separated from one another not less than those who live in different cities, and they learn news of those who dwell near them as they would of those who are living abroad. Indeed they are kept in their houses by rain and hail and snow and winds almost as though they were prisoners, and only the slaves, who have of old learned to endure hardship, dash off bent over to market. So when the weather clears up they greet and embrace one another like people arrived safe from a long voyage, having been forced to neglect, with regard to one another, many things which the law of friendship prescribes, but blaming, instead of themselves, the things by which they were hindered. With us, however, Zeus is not thus; he does not send sharp hail, or thick snow, or heavy rain, by which the even flow of association is broken up. While the year takes its changes from the seasons, association is not altered by any season, but the rain beats upon the roofs, and we, walking about in the stoas at our ease, sit together where we wish. Those who live at the far ends of the side streets are protected by eaves which project from the walls on each side of the street, and these bring them, safe from the rain, to the stoas. So, with other people, the habit of society is dulled in proportion to the distance by which they are separated; with us, friendship grows by the unceasing nature of our association, and here it increases in the same proportion that it declines elsewhere . . . . Just as, at Athens, the most important thing was the desire for knowledge, and honor of it, and acquisition of it, even so with us nothing is beyond being wondered at and everything is inferior to the love of knowledge.

Antioch, like every other city in its world, had changed in many ways since the days of its founder Seleucus. But the figure of Tyche, Good Fortune, which Seleucus had set up soon after founding the city had remained as a symbol which was still in the consciousness of anyone who lived in Antioch or visited the city. Not only did the sculptor Eutychides' figure still stand sheltered under its ornamental stone canopy supported on four pillars, but it had been copied on coins and on glass flasks and on lamps which were manufactured for sale to visitors. The Tyche had remained as a symbol of the city through its many changes of fortune. Whatever vicissitudes it might have passed through, Antioch was still one of the great cities of the world, and "the Good Fortune of Antioch" was not simply a conventional phrase. Visitors were still attracted to the city; as Libanius had written:

> Indeed, if a man had the idea of traveling all over the earth, not to see how cities looked, but to learn their ways, our city would fulfill his purpose and save him his journeying. If he sits in our market place he will sample every city, there will be so many people from each place with whom he can talk. As for those who have chosen this city in preference to their own, it is not to be held against them that they live away from home, but those who have stayed behind envy them, and blame themselves for not having emigrated. Thus a common enjoyment of good things is available to this city. The foreigners cherish as their home the city which they have chosen instead of their homes, while the fellow citizens of these foreigners do not think it meet to gain an advantage over them, but the city loves the virtues of those who come to it exactly as it does the virtues of its own children, imitating the Athenians in this also.

Antioch indeed was in many ways still a polis, a Greek city; and here lay one of its contributions to the future.

CHAPTER V

THE OLD WORLD OF LIBANIUS

*"Literature and the worship
of the gods are twin sisters."*

—LIBANIUS

AS the visitor became acquainted with the city, one of the chief figures that would be pointed out to him was Libanius, the celebrated orator, teacher, and man of letters. Sixty-five years old when the reign of Theodosius opened, and at the height of his great powers, Libanius was recognized without question as the leading citizen of Antioch. This distinction had come to him because of his personal character and his merits and achievement. But Libanius was much more than the first citizen of Antioch. Perhaps neither Libanius himself nor the visitor could have realized at the time the full significance of Libanius' position; but he played a very special part as a representative and champion of the old pagan culture, summing up in himself the problems of the fourth century and bearing the special stamp the century placed on its thinkers and men of letters. In this sense a visit to Antioch would enable the observer to see at firsthand the factors, pagan and Christian, that were involved in this age of transition, for the pagan Libanius and his Christian pupil John Chrysostom embodied in their persons and in their careers the rival forces then at work in the Roman Empire.

The fourth century might be thought of as one of the centuries in antiquity in which some contemporary thinkers

ANTIOCH

were deeply concerned about the motivation and bases of
their society, and concerned and indeed apprehensive about
the future. The reasons for this were of course first, the
emergence of Christianity as a new factor in public life and
a growing factor in private life, and second, the development
of the political, social, and economic changes which were
taking place in the state as a whole as a consequence of the
reforms introduced by Diocletian and Constantine the Great.
It was an era in which contemporary observers were aware
both of peril and of change, and of innovation which sometimes they could only look upon with some misgiving.

It is our good fortune that we are able to see the century
and its problems through the eyes of contemporary observers
of quite different temperaments, and it is thanks to them
that we can learn so much from this singularly interesting
epoch. The religious, social, and political problems of the
century were in fact such that they would call forth different
responses from different people. Libanius, Themistius, the
Emperor Julian, John Chrysostom, Synesius of Cyrene, Eusebius of Caesarea, Basil of Caesarea—these thoughtful men,
with their diverse minds and their diverse passions, show us
an era in which both the old and the new were matters of
immediate, even critical, concern.

In the days of the Emperor Theodosius not everyone in
Antioch, perhaps, thought of the times as critical. Libanius
may sometimes have felt himself alone in his concern for the
pagan way of life; at least he may have felt that he, more
than others, understood the dangers which threatened this
way of life, and the whole life of the state as well.

The bulk of Libanius' written work alone made him seem
a formidable figure. In his own day his literary style was
looked upon as a model, though to some modern readers it
seems involved. But behind this there is a real man, and a

human being of dignity and worth. It is true that Libanius was sometimes irritable, vain, hypochondriacal. But this is by no means an uncommon assortment of characteristics. Libanius was never mean or selfish or petty; he was certainly a kind and generous person, and behind the rhetoric we can see a warm human concern for the young men whose minds it was his task to enlarge and train. Above all, he was intensely patriotic, in the old Greek sense of patriotic devotion to one's city. It was this passionate love for his native city, Antioch, that left its special impress on his whole career.

Vanity; hypochondria, accompanied by some real illnesses; patriotism; love of classical eloquence and of the pagan gods —the observer might, according to his inclination, see Libanius in rather different lights, and some of these might be quite highly colored indeed. But Libanius lived in what were, for him, difficult times, and though by the time of the reign of the Emperor Theodosius he was without any doubt the first citizen of his city, no one could have convinced him that his life had not been a difficult one.

Libanius represented the generation that had grown up after the triumph of Christianity, had had to watch what that meant for paganism, then had witnessed the attempt of Julian at the revival of paganism, and its failure. Of the three great pagan spokesmen of the latter part of the fourth century, Libanius was the oldest, having been born in the year 314. His friend Themistius, the great orator of Constantinople, was born about 317. The future Emperor Julian—the Apostate, or the Philosopher, depending upon one's sympathies—was younger, born in 332. Libanius as a young man would have known men who had lived in a wholly pagan world—his own father, for example. He had ample evidence in his own profession of what the advent of Christianity meant. He had been in touch with Julian and had hoped that Julian's selection of Antioch for his headquarters was a happy omen; but like Julian he had been disappointed in the response of the pagans of Antioch.

Libanius and Themistius were completing their education at the time of the death of Constantine the Great in the year 337. They were not of the preceding generation that witnessed the conversion of Constantine and the emancipation of Christianity, but they had inherited the triumph of the new religion as something that had altered their world. This meant that they had to look at the situation not as a growing threat but as an accomplished fact whose results were already evident. With their younger contemporary Julian they set themselves to live in the new world for which they sometimes did not feel themselves made.

Julian was at once the most highly placed and the most passionate of the three great pagans, and thanks to his royal birth and his imperial office (A.D. 361–63) it was possible for him to undertake to eradicate Christianity not only as a religious abomination but as a threat to the security of the state and of society. Themistius, older than Julian, and placed in a position in which he had to measure carefully what he could do, did not attempt active opposition. Instead he set himself to call attention discreetly to the inherent and continuing values of paganism and to the significance of paganism for contemporary education and society. Paganism, he tried to show, offered values which were comparable to those of Christianity, if not indeed superior. Themistius apparently hoped that if the pagan offering could be appreciated and maintained, at least some of the pagan tradition might be saved. Moreover, Themistius entered earnest and sometimes successful pleas for religious toleration. He even advised Christians to be more tolerant of each other. As all his contemporaries recognized, Themistius was remarkably successful in his discreet campaign, and he was able to maintain an important position at court under a succession of Christian emperors beginning with Constantine's son Constantius (A.D. 337–61). If he was an *aulicus adulator,* "a court flatterer," as he has been called by a modern critic, his flattery had a serious purpose. He was even entrusted with the signal honor of serving as tutor of the son of the most Christian Emperor Theodosius.

Libanius came from a different origin than Julian or Themistius, and the circumstances of his birth and education all pointed to the career which he was to follow so successfully. He was born into a prominent pagan household of Antioch which at one time had been wealthy; it was a respected family that for generations had been distinguished for culture and public spirit. Two of Libanius' uncles were men of means and public position, bearing responsible parts in the public affairs of the city. But it was typical of the Antioch of that day that the family seems not to have been of pure Greek descent; Libanius' own name was not Greek, but contained the common Semitic root *leben,* meaning "white," which appears in the name of the Lebanon Mountains. In this small detail we can see the vitality of Greek culture, which was to find one of its greatest champions in a man who was not of undiluted Greek blood.

When he had completed his classical training in Antioch, Libanius at the age of twenty-two set out for advanced studies in Athens, then still the greatest center in the world for higher training in philosophy and literature, corresponding to a large university center of later times. Here Libanius' natural talent was developed, and he made many friends, including two young Christians, Basil of Caesarea and Gregory of Nazianzus, both later to become bishops and to rank among the most distinguished Christian theologians of their day.

ANTIOCH

After four years at Athens (A.D. 336–40), Libanius went to Constantinople, where he set up on his own as a teacher of rhetoric and soon attracted many students. But the academic world of the imperial capital was poisoned by the intrigues of rival teachers, and Libanius eventually found himself forced to leave. He moved to Nicaea, and after teaching there for a time settled in Nicomedia (A.D. 346), where he remained for five happy years. Then he was encouraged to return to Constantinople, where he remained for a few years before making what was to be his final move, and the one for which he had long been hoping, a permanent removal to his native city (A.D. 354).

Libanius was now forty, and a figure of considerable prestige in the academic world. He had by this time had varied experience in the imperial capital and in two other great cities. All this was in the reign of Constantine's son Constantius—the first reign in which the emperor had been born a Christian. Libanius, as he taught the traditional classical course of studies, came to see that the advent of Christianity was threatening the basis of classical education. Some Christians would not send their children to a pagan teacher, and they would not allow their children to read some of the standard classical authors whose works were not suitable, it was thought, for Christian consumption, such as some of the accounts of the private lives of the gods and goddesses, the plays of Aristophanes, and so on. This must have been a bitter experience for Libanius and his peers. For the present, there were still enough pagan parents to make it possible for a man like Libanius to carry on as a pagan teacher of the classical curriculum, and the imperial administration had at least as yet not taken any official measures against pagan teachers as such; but the pagans, as they saw the Emperor Constantius' Christian zeal and the growing power of the church, must have wondered what was in store for them. This must have been a constant source of anxiety among the pagan professors. They must have followed with interest Themistius' addresses to the Emperor in which he so cleverly and discreetly set out some of the traditional ethical teachings of paganism and their values for education.

Libanius signalized his return to his native city by writing his *Antiochikos* or encomium of Antioch, one of his best-known and most important works. This was written for delivery at the celebration of the Olympic Games of Antioch in the year 356, that is, the first celebration of the games which occurred after his return to Antioch. It is significant that Libanius chose as the occasion for the presentation of the encomium the Olympic Games, attended by visitors from all over the world, as well as—we may be sure—by the entire population of Antioch.

If the *Antiochikos* is read in the light of Libanius' subsequent career in Antioch, it is not difficult to find a clue to what was uppermost in his mind as he took up his work in his beloved native city and prepared to carry on his profession in a world which seemed to be increasingly dominated by the new religion which was hostile to Greek civilization. The *Antiochikos* in fact is a history and encomium of Antioch as a Greek polis, a classical city. It seems clear from the way in which he wrote that Libanius had concluded that his career in his native city should be devoted to keeping alive the tradition of the polis, in all its ancient aspects, as a concept which could be held up against the encroachment and threat of Christianity. Of course Antioch under the Romans was no longer a true polis, socially or politically, but it had been founded as a Greek city and it had a great tradition, and it was this that Libanius set himself to keep alive.

The literary plan of the *Antiochikos* shows what he had

in mind. The first half is concerned with the foundation of Antioch and its history. The remainder is devoted to the topography of the city and its daily life in Libanius' day. The allocation of space in the first section is significant. After a short introduction, several pages are devoted to an account of the land around Antioch. Then a longer section describes the mythological history of the site in the days before the foundation of the city. The mythological fore-runners were some of the most distinguished figures in Greek legend— the Argives under Triptolemus searching for Io, Kasos of Crete, the Herakleidae with the Eleans. This provided a distinguished ancestry for the city.

Libanius then proceeded to describe Alexander the Great's visit to the future site of Antioch, its foundation by Seleucus Nicator in 300 B.C., and the history of the city during the Hellenistic period. Here the emphasis is on the Greek and Macedonian origin of the city. The city was founded by the will of the Greek gods, principally Zeus and Apollo, and the divine favor gave good hope for the prosperity of the new foundation. Through the Athenians who formed a part of the first colonists, the city became the heir of Athens and, as Libanius phrased it, preserved the deeds of the Athenians. Seleucus Nicator as a founder of cities spread Hellenic civilization through the barbarian world and brought barbarism to an end. The history of the Seleucid kings is then detailed. Then, most revealingly, the Romans are dismissed in a couple of paragraphs. When the Macedonian rule came to an end, by divine will, the city accepted the change, Libanius said, because it was a decree of the gods, and handed itself over to the Romans under whose power it was necessary for it to come. In return the Romans treated the city well. Thus good things continued to come to the city and Antioch preserved the place of honor it already possessed, as "metropolis of Asia" (in Libanius' phrase).

Thus Libanius dismissed the Roman history of Antioch politely, but with the least possible amount of attention. One could expect, of course, that his interest would be in the Greek history of the city. But the remainder of the *Antiochikos* shows that it was not merely the Greek history of Antioch that claimed Libanius' attention, but the Greek institutions of the city, as he described them. He began with the senate, upon which, he said, the whole structure of the city was based. The senate was powerful because of its wisdom and its eloquence, and as a consequence Antioch was able to control the officials who were sent out to govern it; in this respect, indeed, Antioch was superior to other cities. (One wonders what the Roman officials who served in Antioch thought of this touch.)

Specifically, it was the "eloquence of Antioch"—meaning the eloquence possessed by its citizens—which Libanius regarded as one of its chief virtues. This eloquence was, he said, rightly called the mind of a city. At Athens the most important thing was the desire for knowledge and the honor of it and the acquisition of it. In the same way, in Antioch, everything was inferior to the love of knowledge. Thus, Libanius said, "just as in former times the fortunes of Greece were divided between two cities, Athens and Sparta, today the fair possessions of the Greeks are divided between two cities, Antioch and Athens"—and here Libanius made the revealing comment that Antioch was to be considered Greek, on a par with Athens, for men were to be called Greeks because of their eloquence rather than their birth. Here Libanius was clearly echoing the famous passage in the *Panegyric* of Isocrates. The great orator of classical Athens and the rhetorician of Roman Antioch both looked to Greek *paideia,* Greek culture, as the norm of civilization.

Libanius closed this part of the discourse with a detailed account of the way in which the eloquence of Antioch arose from its excellence in education—and here, of course, Libanius came to his own profession. He declared that education, the thing which was of all things the most useful, came into the possession of all men at Antioch. The power of the city drew to it strangers who wished to partake of its surpassing education. Those who came to Antioch as rulers became lovers of the city because of its wisdom and its literary distinction, and the people of Antioch itself enjoyed a social life and a kind of intellectual association such as the people of other cities did not. In part, of course, this was because of the physical beauty and the convenience of the city. The remarkably temperate climate and the prosperity of the region combined to make Antioch such a place that it had even convinced Roman visitors that it was superior to what could be found in Italy.

In all this, of course, Libanius was speaking of the city by itself, as an entity, in its historical tradition, and not as a part of the empire or in political relation to it, except in so far as the city by its special virtue could control the officials who were sent to govern it. The *Antiochikos* is in fact a study in what the Greek polis could be even after it had lost its political significance.

What did this mean in relation to actuality at Antioch in Libanius' day? If Libanius could describe Antioch in terms of its past as a great polis, it was certainly no longer a real polis in his own time. The Romans as soon as they had occupied Syria had inaugurated an extensive building program which gave Antioch many of the characteristic features of a Roman city; in fact the Forum of Valens, resembling the

Forum of Trajan in Rome, was to be built during Libanius' own lifetime. The city being the headquarters of the Count of the East and the governor of Syria, there were numbers of Latin-speaking officials and clerks in the city, and there were actually teachers of the Latin language in Antioch—an abomination to Libanius, for here there was a real threat to Greek education.

There were also other elements in Antioch which were foreign to the polis, notably—and very conspicuously—the indigenous Semitic element which had been prominent in Antioch since its foundation. One would not hear Syriac spoken everywhere in the streets of a classical polis. Indeed, many of the Semitic-speaking people in and around Antioch knew no Greek. Aware that his own name was not Greek, Libanius indeed recognized that it was Greek speech and culture which were the criterion of membership in the polis; and he declared, at one point in his *Antiochikos,* "We too have done honor to foreigners in the greatest things, and have profited from foreigners, so that even now their families hold positions among the first."

Such were the accretions to the polis at Antioch—the results of its geographical position and of historical developments. In addition there was the arrival of Christianity, which was the newest threat to the traditional civilization.

Here we come to one of the most characteristic—and at first glance most puzzling—phenomena in the interplay of paganism and Christianity in the fourth century. Highly educated pagans such as Themistius and Libanius appear to have been completely unable to understand the Christian doctrine or to appreciate the Christian way of life; and another learned and sensitive soul, Julian, who had once nominally been a Christian, had changed so much he could only pour scorn on it.

The reason may be found in paganism rather than in Christianity; and it is a commentary on the strength of the classical tradition, and its self-assurance, that men such as Libanius were so hopelessly unable to perceive the significance of Christianity. Classical culture contained the power which enabled it to take sole possession of a mind which had been fully and sympathetically exposed to its genius. In many cases, obviously, Christianity was able to reach into the classically trained mind, but it need not be surprising that in a person such as Libanius the ancient tradition was so strong. Here indeed paganism simply kept its mind closed, so far as Christianity was concerned. Paganism was the established order, and for centuries it had been the only order. The classical credo had its own ancient belief in the dignity and the intrinsic worth of man, a belief which must seem, to the followers of the pagan way, the only possible reason for the existence of the world and of man. If the Christians took a different view of man and of human virtue, this could hardly be right. Had not the traditional belief been proved to be true by generations of good men? If a new way of life put itself forward and sought to establish itself, paganism was bound to resist, and to attack in self-defense; but it did not need to attempt to understand the newcomer, for anything outside the traditional sphere of paganism must by nature be wrong, and not worth understanding. Pagans with little knowledge of Christianity were convinced that theirs was the true way of life and the true perspective on the universe. Why should they trouble with something totally alien, which sought to turn the world upside down? It must be resisted, and if possible suppressed; but the teaching itself need not be studied; it must be erroneous since it was at variance with everything that had gone into the making of the established order. This established order had come into existence, first among the Greeks, then among the Romans, as something that distinguished its possessors from the barbarians who lived outside the boundaries of the civilized world. Thus it was a national heritage as well as a personal allegiance. If it were upset, the nation would lose the basis of its stability.

Thus, with only a partial and probably inaccurate idea of Christianity, Libanius could hardly be expected to appreciate that Antioch was notable as an ancient center of Christianity and that historically this was a city in which the new religion possessed special roots. Libanius could only be aware of the influence that Antioch had exercised and was exercising as a center of pagan culture. What Libanius thought the future would bring—whether he realized that the triumph of Christianity was assured and inevitable—we cannot now venture to say. He did witness Julian's effort at the revival of paganism and the failure of this effort. After the death of Julian, Libanius well may have felt that the future held no further chance of the destruction of Christianity and the return of paganism. For both Libanius and Themistius, Julian's death was the end of an epoch. But neither of them gave up with the disappearance of Julian. They both continued their chosen work, and they had thirty years of active effort before them. Themistius and Libanius were friends and as we noted nearly the same age. If Libanius, on the death of Julian, thought that the cause of paganism now had a limited future, he also knew that Themistius had had a considerable success in his propaganda for paganism in the imperial capital. It must have meant a great deal to both Themistius and Libanius to know that they were not alone in their efforts, and each could draw strength from the success which the other was having. It is characteristic that each of them had developed different interests, though the work of each complemented that of the other. Themistius, at the imperial court, and in constant touch with the successive emperors, was able to view his mission in national terms, while Libanius the professor lived and worked within the framework of the city.

Libanius sought to play his role in two ways, as teacher and as citizen—that is, as teacher of the Greek tradition and as leading citizen and spokesman of the community which preserved the ancient virtues of the polis. The Greek city with Greek culture continued to be, for Libanius, the essential condition of civilized life. The traditional responsibility of the polis for education was something that Libanius, who had soon become one of the leading teachers in the city, could take the lead in upholding. It was his opportunity and privilege to try to teach his pupils, and others, that the virtue and strength of the city, and the virtue which the city gave its citizens, had roots in the past which continued into the present, essentially unaltered in spite of the presence of the Romans and the ill-omened advent of Christianity. The classical spirit, which was the foundation of education and of virtue, still had to manifest itself through the city. The Emperor Julian had characteristically thought in terms of the traditional concept of the polis and its role. The ideal of citizenship, to him, was to be the most virtuous man in the city; and in the face of the Christian threat, Julian wrote, pagans should honor both the men and the cities which revered the gods. If it is said that Libanius lived in the past, this meant that he devoted himself to trying to show that the past was an essential part of the present and offered to the present the virtues it had bestowed in the past. Libanius could teach this to his pupils, and by his public speeches he could try to preserve the independence of Antioch from the effects of the imperial regime as this had been developing in Libanius' lifetime.

Libanius was constantly on the watch to preserve justice in society and in government, and he wrote a whole series of speeches, either as addresses to the emperor or to the imperial governors, or as pamphlets or open letters, which reveal both his warm humanity and his concern for the maintenance of decency and order in the life of the human beings who collectively composed the polis Antioch.

There were many needs that claimed his attention. Penal reform was one of the most urgent, and in a famous discourse *Concerning the Prisoners* he pleaded for better treatment of prisoners awaiting trial and for more prompt hearings of the accused, as well as for fairer administration of justice when the accused were able to have a trial. According to the laws in force, these evils need not have existed; it was from the laziness, incompetence, and venality of the judges and the officials of the courts and prisoners that the abuses stemmed. Conditions in Antioch had become such that Libanius thought it necessary to address this discourse to the Emperor; and the legislation issued by Theodosius does indicate that Libanius' exposition had some effect.

Not only prisoners, but the poor and the working classes needed support and protection, and Libanius often intervened to seek just treatment for all those who were in danger of being exploited by interests which were more powerful than they—farmers, bakers, small tradesmen. An imperial governor who failed to carry out his duties properly could expect to find his shortcomings detailed in an "open letter" which was read by everyone in Antioch; and if a controversy arose, it was Libanius who through his prestige and his literary gifts had the advantage.

Indeed Libanius was quick to note any plan, any innovation, which seemed to contain a threat to the ideal way of life in Antioch, and an open letter or public speech would follow. If the banquets which concluded the Olympic Games were losing their traditional character because guests were being allowed to bring their sons when the boys were still too young to be able to take part properly in such an occasion, Libanius felt that this was a matter of public concern to the whole city, for the fitting celebration of the games was an important manifestation of the true life of the city. Another threat to the integrity of the games was the effort to enlarge the Plethrion, the building in which the athletes who sought to enter the games went through their trials and elimination contests. The building had originally been small enough so that only the officials concerned and some of the more responsible citizens might witness these contests. An enlargement would admit a crowd of idlers and persons of undesirable character who ought not to be present; and here again Libanius saw the need for a public protest against an innovation which would cheapen the games.

In spite of his recurrent headaches and frequent illnesses, Libanius labored unceasingly for the maintenance of order and decorum in the life of his city. In this he not only maintained his role of first citizen, but carried out his function as teacher, in giving his pupils an example of citizenship embodying the virtues of the classical polis as these could be brought to bear on contemporary problems.

Libanius and his friends, and the pupils whom he influenced so deeply, were conscious, and keenly conscious, of the role of the past in the formation of the present, and it was in the preservation of the noble tradition of the past that they saw the assurance of the future. This was Libanius' guiding thought as he watched the life of Antioch around him. Innovation was not in itself necessarily a bad thing; but it might be highly dangerous if it displaced something of tried and permanent value with a new order of questionable worth. The world, Libanius saw, was full of these impulses to change and novelty and "improvement." But what would emerge if all these forces were allowed free play, unscrutinized and unchecked?

It was not so much forces of change as forces of decline that Libanius feared. If the true life of society centered in the city could be maintained, decline could be prevented. Libanius' concern for the polis was so deep because it was here, under the pressure of the Christian challenge, and in the light of current political developments, that he saw one of the real motivations of life—that is, the pagan polis, with its long historical tradition, its gods, its educational responsibility, the virtues which it bred in its citizens. In all the menaces to civilization and society which Libanius saw all around him, he perceived threats to the tradition of the polis. Indeed it was as this threat increased that Libanius saw more and more clearly what the polis stood for. In spite of his courage Libanius saw his world declining. Libanius might even have borrowed a phrase from Gibbon and traced this decline to the triumph of barbarism and the Christian religion. What Libanius did not understand was that the forces in motion were really different from what he imagined them to be, and that they were stronger than he supposed. Not understanding the mainspring of these forces, he could not realize what it was that they were developing. One of the pagan objections to Christianity was that this new religion seemed to discredit and indeed eliminate the past as the essential formative tradition on which the established civilization was built. What Libanius and his friends did not realize was that Christianity had substituted a new conception of the reason of life, and that the Christian view of nature, man, and God represented a force that was to transform society.

The basic element in either view of society and the world, pagan or Christian, was still man. Classical Greece had been a civilization of the person, and Christianity was a religion of the transformation of the person. Libanius, as he sat in his school, or walked along the colonnaded streets, could think only in terms of one kind of person. It was this kind of person that he believed must survive if civilization was to be preserved. What he did not realize was that his beloved type of person might be absorbed within the new Christian ideal, so that the classical tradition might find a new and continuing life within the new Christian culture. At this very time Christian theologians and philosophers were working toward this end. And it was the peculiar strength of classical humanism that kept Libanius from seeing this.

CHAPTER VI

JOHN CHRYSOSTOM'S NEW WORLD

"The love of Christ controls us."

—II CORINTHIANS

IF the visitor climbed Mount Silpius and studied the city stretched out before him, he would see more pagan temples than Christian churches. But the temples, he knew, were now little more than historic monuments and museums, for if Antioch was an ancient home of the gods, it was also the place in which the disciples had first been called Christians. No one, pagan or Christian, could forget this, for in the whole panorama of the city, the most arresting feature was the golden dome of Constantine the Great's octagonal Great Church, completed forty years previously, standing in its spacious colonnaded courtyard surrounded by various buildings designed for the service of the church. This was the greatest Christian shrine in the city; but there was also rising a new church, built in the past few years and not yet completed. This was the cruciform Church of St. Babylas situated on the other side of the Orontes from the city, there being no more room in the city itself for such a large edifice. It was appropriate, too, to build the church on the Campus Martius where so many Christian martyrs had been executed, for Babylas, Bishop of Antioch, had been a celebrated martyr, indeed one of the earliest and greatest martyrs of the city.

To the Christian visitor, the spectacle of temples and churches would tell the story of the fame of Antioch as an early and vigorous center of Christianity. The long Christian tradition, now triumphant after three centuries of being outlawed, was embodied in Constantine's church, the cathedral of the patriarchate of Antioch, in which every Christian visitor to Antioch would hasten to worship.

Here the stranger would hear John Chrysostom, the celebrated preacher whose reputation was extending well beyond his native city. If the visitor knew of Libanius as a last representative of the culture of old Athens, John Chrysostom was becoming famous as one of the great prophets of the life of the New Jerusalem.

As he stood up to preach from the ambon or marble pulpit in the center of the octagonal church, John Chrysostom seemed outwardly a far from distinguished figure. Slight in stature, he looked thin, even in his vestments, with emaciated features and a high, bald forehead. Everyone in Antioch knew that his self-imposed fasts, when he had retired to the desert as a young man to engage in contemplation, had damaged his digestion. He ate only enough to keep himself alive, and it was said that he suffered from constant dyspepsia. He was truly, in the common phrase, an "athlete of Christ," for everything in his bearing and appearance spoke of the rigorous spiritual training he had imposed upon himself; and among the Christians of that day these marks commanded great respect, just as in an earlier time the bodily tokens of the confessors of the faith—an eye missing, a lame leg, a crippled hand, signs of the tortures they had endured for the sake of the Gospel—gave them commanding stature among their fellow Christians.

If you had passed John Chrysostom in the street, you would hardly have noticed him. At most you would have noted a frail, rather shabby priest. But when, part of the service of the Eucharist being completed, this preacher made his way to the pulpit and began to speak, every man and woman in the congregation knew that this was an experience that did not often occur. It was no wonder that John of Antioch soon came to be known as John Chrysostom, "John of the Golden Mouth." For he had the gift of glorious eloquence, a gift such as not many preachers of the Word before or after him possessed.

The deeply religious mind, the acute and sensitive knowledge of the human soul, the wide and penetrating learning in the Scriptures, and above all, the passionate devotion to the teaching of Christ—all this was magnificently poured forth in a stream of eloquence which would have made him one of the most powerful speakers of the time, whether in a pagan career or a Christian vocation. It was the gift of language in its greatest and noblest dimension, and when it was known that John Chrysostom was to preach, the cathedral was packed. The farmers who came in from the country around Antioch, and the humblest workingmen of the city, who understood only Syriac, were grouped at one side of the church, around a deacon, bilingual in Greek and Syriac, who translated the sermon sentence by sentence as it was spoken. A team of shorthand writers took down the preacher's words, for he often spoke extemporaneously, as inspiration came to him. Though the sermon sometimes lasted for two hours, the congregation—standing all the while—never grew weary, and the stenographic reports often record the interruptions of applause which were permitted by custom at that time.

John Chrysostom felt, and rightly, that his true vocation was that of a pastor of souls—and it was as such that people flocked to hear him. As his principal vehicle for his message—instruction, admonition, consolation, exhortation—he chose Biblical sermons in which the books of the Old and New Testaments were systematically expounded. These discourses were usually delivered in a continuous series, in which a selected book—Genesis, Psalms, Isaiah, Matthew, John, Acts, Romans, Corinthians, other epistles—was studied systematically and at length. Each verse was quoted and elucidated, and its purpose discovered. No aspect of the thought of the writer was left unnoticed, and the interpretations were often arresting in their simplicity and directness.

Everything in Chrysostom's thought and discourse was directed to the examination of the dialogue between God and man. The preacher spoke directly to the hearts of his congregation, and there seemed to be no part of their lives, and no kind of trial, burden, temptation, or sorrow—or, indeed, joy—that he did not know. It was his accurate and compassionate knowledge of humanity—seen always in the context of divine love—which as much as anything gave him his enormous prestige. Everyone knew that the preacher's every thought was directed toward the spiritual upbuilding of his flock, toward filling their needs and showing them their true nature and true vocation as children of God. There seemed no facet of the spiritual life of man he did not know, and no spiritual need of his people he did not know how to deal with. The whole Christian population of Antioch looked upon him with affection, sometimes with a feeling of awe, and even the pagans respected his easy and elegant command of the Greek language.

As he listened, the visitor might wonder what had gone to make this singular messenger of the Word. Obviously it was the hand of God at work; but what would be the earthly preparation for such a career?

The preacher's birth and parentage had not, indeed, been

significantly different from those of a number of his contemporaries in Antioch. His parents were Christians and occupied a position of some importance and responsibility in Antioch. His father, a man of noble birth and some property, had begun a successful career in the imperial civil service, and through his ability had come to a responsible position in the office of the Count of the East while he was still a relatively young man. But in those days of limited medical resources, the father died suddenly, leaving his widow Anthusa with their son John, an infant.

This was a far from uncommon situation, and the young widow—she was twenty years old—set about to devote herself to her son's education. Some widows might have been forced by economic needs to remarry; but fortunately there was enough property so that Anthusa did not have to do this. It was possible indeed to send the boy to the best teachers in Antioch, and he was taught philosophy by Andragathius and literature and rhetoric by Libanius.

The boy's education uncovered a notable talent for literature and rhetoric, and—again like many of his contemporaries—John planned to use his gifts in the civil service in which his father had been successful. For this he would need to study law after his training in rhetoric was completed.

But while he was studying under his pagan professors, the boy, under his mother's guidance, was performing his Christian duties, and at the age of eighteen he experienced a conversion, literally a turning toward God, such as he had not previously known. John Chrysostom did not record the circumstances of his transformation, but the young man—the age of eighteen in Syria brought a measure of maturity of mind—now knew what his vocation as a Christian was to be. His talent and his personal gifts had already brought him to the notice of Meletius, the bishop of Antioch, and the bishop, perceiving what this young man might become, added him to the circle of students whom he kept about him. There were no theological seminaries at that time, and the bishops gathered around themselves young men of promise who might be expected to seek ordination, and gave them such instruction as they found opportunity to provide.

To the young John, this was a wonderful opportunity, and his faith grew and deepened under the teaching and the personal influence of the Bishop. The young man progressed to the point at which he was ready to receive baptism, and after three years of attendance on the Bishop he was advanced to be anagnost or reader, a minor order in the church, so that he regularly took part in the service, reading responses and chanting prayers.

John now began to study not only with the Bishop but with the famous theologian Diodorus of Tarsus, a learned monk who had settled in a monastery in Antioch and had attracted pupils by his scholarship and piety. All this time John was living at home, but in a strictly ascetic fashion, eating sparingly, sleeping as little as possible, and devoting all his time to study and prayer.

Soon John came to think of taking what was often the next step, a withdrawal from the world into the desert or into a cave in the mountainside above Antioch where he might devote himself to prayer and contemplation, freed from the distractions of the world. To reach the heights of spirituality, one must be free from earthly temptations. But his mother besought him not to make her a widow once more, leaving her with the entire responsibility for the management of the household and the property.

But the young man felt the pull of his vocation so strongly that he did after all retire from the world, and doubtless his mother perceived that this had to be. In the mountains near

Antioch he found an old hermit named Syrus, living in a cave, and in his company the young man spent four years, learning wisdom from the hermit and schooling himself to master his passions and the pull which the world must inevitably have for any young man in the full powers of his youth. The mastery of the flesh, by solitary life, meager diet, and constant prayer, was the normal training for a young man entering on the religious life.

John's biographer Palladius writes that when at length he found it more easy to master the temptations to pleasure, "not so much by toil as by reason, he retired to a cave by himself, in his eagerness to hide himself from the world, and there spent twenty-four months, for the greater part of which he denied himself sleep, while he studied the Covenants of Christ [i.e., the Old and the New Testaments], the better to dispel ignorance. Two years spent without lying down by night or day deadened his gastric organs, and the functions of the kidneys were impaired by the cold." Then, finding that he could not doctor himself, and understanding that he should not sacrifice his life in this fashion, he returned to Antioch.

As he had hoped, John came back to Antioch wholly changed within, and now, having mastered himself and brought all his forces and his thoughts under the control of his vision of Christ, he felt prepared to dedicate himself to the service of God. First, however—like many young men of his time—he felt the need of a further period of study, and he hoped to spend his time in contemplation and discourse with a friend of the same age and the same background, Basil. But the Bishop and his clergy had long been watching John Chrysostom, for they saw what gifts he had, and John was at length brought to yield. He was ordained deacon in 381 by his friend Bishop Meletius, and was advanced to the priesthood five years later by Meletius' successor, Bishop Flavian. Flavian appointed him to the staff of the cathedral, where he would preach and take part in the diverse pastoral activities which had grown up about the principal church of the city.

As he looked about him, John saw the many and varied needs for the Christian ministry in the Antioch of that day. It was only something like seventy years since the faith had been emancipated by Saint Constantine the Great, and while the new era saluted by the Christians of Constantine's reign had certainly arrived, it had not yet by any means reached fulfillment. Paganism had not at all disappeared; indeed the old religion had proved surprisingly tenacious in many parts of the empire, and Antioch had continued to be one of the chief centers of the ancient cults. The Emperor Theodosius had issued a series of edicts forbidding pagan worship and the practice of magic and divination, but while these were enforced for a time after they were issued, there proved to be too many powerful pagans left in the empire, and the edicts became dead letters. Paganism was too deeply rooted to be brought to an end by mere laws. So while John Chrysostom's city was also an ancient home of the Christian faith, the task of making disciples of all men was by no means completed there.

And so the Christian community, its members proud of their spiritual descent from the disciples who first bore the name of Christians, still had to live in a great city in which there were reminders on every side of the pagan way of life. Indeed Christians and pagans had perforce to live in the same world, sharing the same material culture and many of the same daily labors and avocations. The Christian life, as Chrysostom himself knew from his own experience, in itself made sufficient demands on human nature. All Christians were not given equal strength, and when the Christian had to live in the midst of the distractions and temptations of the old pagan world, there was, everyone knew, great peril to the soul. The conversion of the pagan, the fortification of the Christian—this was a formidable task for the priests of John Chrysostom's day. The conversion of the pagan was not alone a matter of moral improvement. What set Christians off from pagans, and what constituted the chasm for the pagans, was that Christians were not just living a better life, they were living a different one.

John Chrysostom had grown up during the Arian controversy—the dispute over the nature of Christ—which had split the whole Greek-speaking part of the empire. Was Christ the Son of God, of the same substance as God the Father, or was he a subordinate creature, created by the Father, superior in nature to men, but still inferior in rank and divinity to the Father? This had been the question proposed sixty-five years earlier by the Egyptian priest Arius. Was Christ divine or was he simply a man—of unusual holiness, but still a man? It was a vital question because it affected the salvation of mankind. Redemption and salvation brought by a Christ who was truly the Son of God, of the same substance and divinity as God the Father, was totally different from a salvation offered by a holy man who, though a special creation of God, was not of the same divine rank.

This was the most formidable question the church had ever faced, and it was one which brought out all the passions of the protagonists. When it assumed the proportions of a threat to public order, the Emperor Constantine summoned the Council of Nicaea in 325 to deal with it. At the council the orthodox defenders of the full divinity of Christ won, but the Arians had their own strength and their own resources, and the controversy continued to rage for sixty-five years under eight emperors, until finally the great theologians of Cappadocia, Basil the Great, his brother Gregory of Nyssa, and their friend Gregory of Nazianzus, gradually by their studies and writings established the orthodox position in terms which could not be shaken. The Emperor Theodosius, himself a devout orthodox Christian, convoked a council at Constantinople in 381 at which the bishops of the church promulgated a creed—later, paradoxically, known as the Nicene Creed—which set forth the orthodox doctrine; and Theodosius, to match the work of the council, issued two imperial edicts which made heresy a crime punishable by human as well as by divine power.

So John took up his career at a time when this savage dispute had at last been settled; but the controversy was remembered all too vividly, and there were still onetime adherents of Arius who could not feel themselves truly reconciled to the orthodox doctrine, and these might find some other leader whose teaching might draw them. John Chrysostom and his older contemporaries remembered the time when the people of Antioch—a stronghold of Arianism— talked of nothing else. Another Christian theologian, disgusted with the constant argumentation he heard on every side, wrote that "Every market place buzzes with the talking of these people, and every dinner party is worried to death by their silly talk; women's apartments in the houses are thrown into confusion."

Some of his fellow Christians, John Chrysostom reflected, had really not understood all that the controversy had involved; and now, because emancipated Christianity was still working out the formulation of its belief, there was arising a dispute over the nature of the Holy Spirit which threatened to be almost as difficult as the earlier Christological problem had been. The bishops at Constantinople had reaffirmed the

Nicene dogma of the divinity of Christ; but now, having established the true nature of the Second Person of the Trinity, they saw that it was necessary to clear up any doubts that existed concerning the Third Person.

The nature of the Holy Spirit had indeed been a question that many quite devout Christians had had difficulty in understanding. Was the Holy Spirit to be thought of as an operation or manifestation of the power of God the Father, or a manifestation of Christ—as sent by Christ—or was it (or he) a true member of the Trinity, equal in all respects, divinity included? The action of the Holy Spirit in their lives was familiar to many Christians, and it was all the more important to know precisely what the Spirit was.

Such was the new controversy which followed inevitably on the Arian dispute. Here again the great Cappadocian theologians were at work, writing learned treatises and polemics, while John Chrysostom was setting out on his career; and while any devout Christian must be resolved to maintain the full divinity of the Spirit, the study was full of difficulties as the opposing parties—those who made the Spirit a creature and those who made him a full member of the Trinity —found scriptural texts which could be quoted in support of their arguments.

This was the theological situation, the intellectual setting of the Christian world, that John Chrysostom found when he returned to Antioch from his excursion into the solitary life. But as he thought of the theological disputation, and looked all around him at the life of the Christian community of Antioch and its immediate practical problems, it seemed to him that, for himself at least, there could be no question. He had been carefully instructed in theology, and he had spent six years in secluded contemplation of the mysteries of God; but as between theological scholarship and the calling of a pastor, there was no possible doubt. The Christians of Antioch would be his life. With men like Basil and the Gregories at work, the purity of the faith would be safe; but here in Antioch, his beloved native city, there was work upon which he understood he could not turn his back. It was the priest's responsibility to fit himself to know what was the will of God for his work, and what it was that was given to him to do. God revealed his purpose, if one knew how to listen for the revelation.

For the priest such as John Chrysostom who had the opportunity and the talent, the career in a city such as Antioch divided itself into two fields, the spiritual and the practical, the didactic and the mundane—though of course all aspects of Christian life were really one and the wise and gifted priest must bring the two together.

From his youth John Chrysostom had felt an urge to teach, and now, as he looked about him in Antioch, he saw how much Christian teaching was needed—teaching of all kinds and at all levels. There was to begin with the sermon, perhaps the most fruitful opportunity for the proclamation of the Word, and at the same time by no means an easy medium. The congregation of the Great Church of Antioch included Christians of every level of education, from the Count of the East and the governor of Syria and the local senators down to the illiterate farmers, artisans, and slaves. Some of the women in the congregation were well educated, some not. There also might be, inconspicuous in the congregation, pagan inquirers who had come to learn something of the Christian belief. All these people—and not least those who were most powerful in the world—needed instruction in the teaching of the church and in Christian living. Some of them needed first of all to be taught to pray and to read the Bible. Some did not own a Bible, or owned only portions of it, and even of these one could not be sure they read it every day. Here was a task that appealed both to John Chrysostom's rhetorical sense and to his Christian love. His sermons had to be planned so that they might offer something to each of his hearers, and here John learned the art of the simplicity which makes the great sermon.

But the task, John knew, was not simply the exposition of the Scriptures and the Christian education of the congregation—who often received no other religious teaching. One of the great needs was for moral instruction. The Christians were living side by side with their pagan fellow citizens—sometimes actually their own relatives—whose culture from ancient times had taught that the end of man on earth was physical enjoyment and material success, and that the human body was a delightful instrument of pleasure.

Here was an area in the life of Antioch on which John was well qualified to speak. He was old enough to remember the reign of Julian the Apostate and the attempt at the pagan revival. He had gone through all the stages of the classical curriculum himself, reading the pagan authors, and studying their style, and many of his companions at school had been pagans. In a city such as Antioch which had originally been pagan, there were signs everywhere of the old way of life, in the public buildings, in the baths and private houses, where paintings, mosaics, and statues depicted scenes of pagan mythology and of the pleasures of contemporary life. Many nominally Christian families kept up pagan customs, such as music and dancing and all manner of merrymaking at weddings, which actually should have been purely religious occasions. Some Christians in fact continued to wear pagan magical objects, and Chrysostom in one of his addresses to converts being instructed for baptism inveighed against "those who use charms and amulets, and encircle their heads and feet with golden coins of Alexander of Macedon." Chrysostom knew well that the local Olympic Games, though purged of the features most objectionable to Christian ideas, were still a pagan festival. Every three years, in May, recurred the festival of the Maiuma with its indescribable orgies by night. Perhaps worst of all, in John Chrysostom's view, because it was a daily occurrence, was the theatre, where ballets and pantomimes depicted the unrestrained private lives of the gods and goddesses. It would not be difficult, the preacher knew, for these shows to undermine the Christian character of some of his flock, and he constantly warned against these delights of the world in the strongest possible terms. At least Chrysostom could be glad that the gladiatorial shows were no longer presented in Antioch in Theodosius' reign. It was not easy for a Christian preacher to compete with the distractions and pleasures of a pagan city such as Antioch, but John Chrysostom realized that this was one of the greatest of the tasks and opportunities that lay before him. His instincts as teacher and pastor were sharpened by what he saw in the society about him. Things that to the pagan were elegant and delightful, to the Christian might very well have a touch of sordidness. It might not be altogether a bad thing for Christianity to have to live to a certain extent in a context of paganism, for this juxtaposition showed how Christian life differed from pagan life. Thoughtful Christians could perceive this, and the skillful pastor of souls could make it the point of his teaching.

But there were other kinds of teaching, in some ways of a more special character, which were also needed. One of John Chrysostom's principal tasks was the instruction of adult converts to Christianity who were being prepared for baptism and reception into the church. This instruction required a very special talent, for the converts came from all suppressed, was being succeeded by troublesome controversy over the Holy Spirit. The visitor from the future would be assured that the political outlook was favorable. Were not the church and the government working together in harmony for the salvation of the people of the empire? The development seemed to be what was wished. Theodosius had been able to accomplish, in religious politics, what Constantine had doubtless hoped for but had not been in a position to effect. Religious harmony, now assured by the police powers of the state, would guarantee the material prosperity as well as the spiritual happiness of the Roman people, for God would look kindly upon all the affairs of his subjects when they were at peace with one another. Thus all the people of the empire, whatever their station or occupation, could go about their daily tasks knowing that they were under the assured protection of the divine favor.

If any official of Theodosius', ecclesiastical or secular, had any doubt about what the future would bring, he must have kept it to himself; and here the visitor, knowing the future, might wonder whether the observers of Theodosius' day might anticipate the times of Justinian, 150 years later, when an able and energetic sovereign carried the evolution of the Christian monarchy to the point at which the emperor, acting independently of any ecclesiastical agency, himself issued pronouncements on dogma which, coming from his sacred person, had the force of law. By the time this happened, the great age of Antioch would have passed; but no one in Antioch in the days of Theodosius could know that 150 years later the city would be ruined by fire, earthquakes, and devastation by the Persians—any more than one could have known, in the time of Libanius and Chrysostom, that less than a century after Justinian's death Antioch would be walks of life and represented every variety of education and religious background. There were philosophers who had been attached to no particular cult, and there were devotees of all the cults then known in the pagan world. Sometimes there were Jews. Some of the converts were obviously sincere; in other cases it was legitimate to wonder whether the newcomers might be entering the church for other than purely religious motives.

All of these converts, then, had to be instructed in the fundamentals of the faith, and their questions had to be answered. One had to be prepared to deal with inquiries and possible objections based on all the schools of philosophy. Sometimes, if the numbers undergoing instruction were large enough, one could divide the candidates into groups according to their background or their proficiency in the faith, but often they had to be taken all together, and then the address of the catechist or instructor had to be very carefully planned indeed. Baptism was administered at Epiphany and on Easter eve, and the rite was followed as well as preceded by instruction.

Baptism was for the most part given to adults; but the instruction of children was considered one of the most necessary and most important parts of the church's teaching. John Chrysostom developed a skill and an insight that made this one of the most effective phases of his ministry.

The treatise which John wrote on the subject reveals his exceptional gift with children, and his understanding of their needs. Chrysostom wrote his discourse for the benefit of parents, for he was especially concerned to show that the most important part of a child's education was received at home. Children were taken to church from an early age, and the parents who could afford to do so sent their children to school; but it was still the work of the parents that to

Chrysostom seemed paramount. He opened with the formative years in which the parents by their own interests and
their desires for the child begin to shape its growth. Some,
he said, may think that these things are trifles, but they are
actually of the first importance. "If good things [Chrysostom
wrote] are impressed on the soul while it is yet tender, no
man will be able to destroy them when they have set firm,
even as does a waxen seal. The child is still trembling and
fearful and afraid in look and speech and in all else. Make
use of the beginning of his life as thou shouldest. Thou wilt
be the first to benefit, if thou hast a good son, and then God.
Thou dost labor for thyself." Parents, like sculptors and
painters, must give all their leisure to fashioning these wonderful statues of God, their children. The senses—the eyes,
the tongue, the hearing, the sense of smell, the sense of touch
—all are the gates which guard the city which is the child's
soul, and these senses must be trained and disciplined.

Everything said to the child makes an impression upon it.
"Let children then hear nothing harmful from servants or
tutor or nurses." Therefore they should not be told frivolous
stories. John Chrysostom knew well the kind of romantic
tales that were in circulation: "This youth kissed that maid-
en. The king's son and the younger daughter have done
this." Instead of such tales, the parents can tell the child well-
known stories from the Old Testament, taking care to make
the stories agreeable, and telling them so that the child may
see the meaning himself. The child's mother should sit by
while the father is telling the story, so that she may praise the
tale and ask suitable questions. Then the parents may take
the child to church where he can hear the same stories read
as part of the service. The child will leap with pleasure because he knows what the other children do not know. He

recognizes all the details of the tale as it is read by the priest or deacon, and it is indelibly fixed on his memory.

Children should be named, not for their forebears, but for martyrs, bishops, and apostles. Thus they will have a constant incentive to imitate the saints for whom they are named.

Thus the child will learn to live in his household and will imitate his parents in their conduct toward one another and toward their slaves. All this is no mere theory, Chrysostom declared: "I am not speaking of trifles; we are discussing the governance of the world." Chrysostom recommended early marriage, before the young man has taken up his career in the army or in political life. If the youth as well as the bride comes to marriage when he is still virtuous, "Will not then the charm of their love be wholly pure? Above all, will not God then be the more gracious and fill that marriage with countless blessings, when they come together according to His ordinances? And He makes the youth remember his love always. And if he is held fast in this affection, he will spurn every other woman." Such was the ideal that Chrysostom set before the Christian parents of Antioch.

But preaching and teaching did not form the whole of John Chrysostom's life. As a member of the staff of the Great Church, it was his responsibility to take an active part in the charitable work which centered about all churches in those days, and more especially about the chief church in each city. In the days of the pagan Roman Empire it was felt, as one of the accepted facts of life, that the state and its secular authorities, both local and imperial, had no responsibility for the systematic relief of poverty and unemployment, or for the medical care of the sick poor. The imperial authorities did provide generous relief after great public disasters, such as earthquakes and famines, but the economic system which created a large class of people who were inevitably poor and unemployed offered no regular provision for their maintenance.

In addition, the limited powers of medicine and the primitive arrangements for public sanitation meant a high mortality rate. Young married men—for example, John Chrysostom's own father—might die of gastric attacks which centuries later would be recognized as appendicitis and successfully treated. Pneumonia was then often, perhaps nearly always, fatal. Epidemics of disease could not be checked—two hundred years before Chrysostom's time the empire had been ravaged by smallpox, the cause and treatment of which were unknown—and it was not an unusual occurrence for a husband and wife to die at the same time. Inevitably any large city such as Antioch had a considerable community of widows, young and old, and orphans, and it was a major responsibility of the church to care for them. In the world of that time it was virtually impossible for these women and children to obtain any employment at all, and they must be guarded against exploitation and against temptations.

The practical problems were numerous and difficult, and Chrysostom learned to deal with them. In the first place money had to be raised to provide the food and clothing for many people for whom the church formed the only means of support. In the courtyard surrounding the Great Church there were kitchens in which meals were cooked for the poor, and the deacons and employees in charge of the kitchens had to be eternally on the watch to eject from the lines of waiting people those who were not really qualified for relief, or who had already passed through the line on the same day. All this cost money, and the clergy had the greatest difficulty in persuading their congregations to make even the modest offerings which were necessary for the support of this essential charity.

How sad to have to beg for money for such causes in one of the wealthiest cities in the world!

Along with its care for widows and orphans and for the poor and the sick, the church felt an obligation for the care of strangers and travelers. Inns were not only expensive but dangerous places for many people to stay in. Guests were liable to be robbed, and the women servants were often prostitutes. Traveling Christians should not be exposed to such accommodations, and the church throughout the empire provided hostels for strangers and visitors, attached to the churches in all the cities and villages in which they could be maintained. In a place such as Antioch, people of humble station had to come to the great city on private business or, when they had legal business, to present petitions to the authorities. It was convenient, too, for the police to be able to know who the visitors were and to keep an eye on their activities. So care for travelers was another public service of the Great Church at Antioch.

The routine maintenance of all these services meant that the clergy of the Great Church had to be able to deal with problems of finance and supply. But if the material needs of this special and changing congregation called for special talents, their spiritual care presented formidable problems with which John Chrysostom became well acquainted. In his treatise *On the Priesthood*, in which the duties of the clergy are described in detail, Chrysostom wrote on these problems evidently from expert knowledge: "Again, in the accommodation of strangers, and the care of the sick, think how great an expenditure of money is needed, and how much exactness and discretion on the part of those who are in charge of these matters. For it is often necessary to lay out considerable sums, and the priest who is in charge should combine prudence and wisdom with skill in the art of supply, so as to dispose the well-to-do to be ungrudging with their gifts, and at the same time avoid vexing them. But there is need of even greater devotion and skill, for the sick are difficult creatures to please, and apt to be listless, and any neglect of the care which is due them may cause harm to them."

Among the orphans, the young unmarried women, because of their unprotected position, were in great danger; women of dubious character came among the young women, and as a result these orphans might come into dangerous situations. The older women presented their special problems. At home, as one visited them, or when they came to church, they were always full of their troubles. Chrysostom painted a lively picture: "The widows have gotten into a common habit of trifling, and railing at one another. They either flatter people, or they are impudent." Unlike respectable women, who spend their time at home engaged in their proper duties, the widows "appear everywhere in public and spend their time walking about the public squares." Such were some of the cares of the pastor. But it was true that in Chrysostom's time women were gaining an increasing influence in the affairs of the church, and the ways in which they made their contribution were many and varied.

Such were the daily tasks—and opportunities—of a pastor in Antioch. In a city of such size there were special calls as well upon the pastor, and special dangers to be faced. One source of trouble to the Christian community in John Chrysostom's time was the attraction Judaism had been exercising for some Christians, especially women. It was, indeed, in the first year after his ordination that Chrysostom was called upon to warn his congregation against this danger. Some

Christians, distressed or puzzled by the theological controversies, were drawn by the simple monotheistic faith of the Jews; others were attracted by the reports of miraculous cures performed by the relics of the Maccabean martyrs, the heroic Jews who had died for their faith under Antiochus IV. The relics, preserved in a synagogue in Antioch which later was made into a Christian church, were thought to have the curative powers often displayed by the remains of martyrs. Inevitably a cult grew up about the relics, and this formed a grave temptation and danger to Christians whose faith was not firmly anchored. Other Christians were attracted by the Jewish ritual and impressed by Jewish piety, especially as shown by the religious fasts. Chrysostom in his sermons endeavored to point out that Christians could only be led astray by these aspects of the Jewish religion if their knowledge of the Christian teaching itself was faulty.

An even graver emergency came upon the whole of Antioch during the second year after Chrysostom's ordination, and here John and his fellow priests found a great opportunity to aid and comfort the people of the city. By the year A.D. 387 "hard times" were being felt throughout the empire. Taxes had had to be increased in order to pay for the rebuilding of the army which had been shattered at the battle of Adrianople nine years earlier, when the Emperor Valens had been defeated and killed by the Goths. Land which had formerly produced income and provided revenue had been ruined by the wars, and the Emperor Theodosius found it necessary to spend increasing amounts on the defense of the empire against the barbarians.

Thus when an imperial edict arrived at Antioch in the early days of February, A.D. 387, announcing an increase in taxes, the reaction was sharp. The people of Antioch had always been accustomed to speak their minds freely to their sovereigns, and they regarded it as their right to explode when they thought they were being pushed too far. When the edict arrived, the municipal senators were as was customary summoned to the *dikasterion*, the law court, where imperial communications were officially published by being read aloud by a herald—a relic of earlier times when most people were illiterate. This time, when the senators heard the news, there was immediate resistance. It would be intolerable to pay the money that was demanded. The senators set out for the residence of Celsus, the governor of Syria, to demand that he have the tax reduced. But they got no satisfaction from Celsus, who had no doubt anticipated this request. Then—such was the prestige of a Christian bishop at this time—they went to the residence of Bishop Flavian. The Bishop, as it proved, was elsewhere—a most unfortunate coincidence, for if he had been able to talk with the senators, he might have been able to prevent what happened later.

By this time a crowd had collected and, as so easily happened on such occasions, some dubious characters appeared and took charge. The crowd turned into a mob. Back they went to the residence of the Governor. The servants and guards had barricaded the mansion, for another Governor, Theophilus, had been killed by a mob thirty-four years previously during a famine. The mob assaulted the door, but could not break it down. Then the rioters rushed along the portico which stood in front of the law court, stopping on the way to invade a public bath where some of the roughs amused themselves by cutting the ropes suspending the hanging lamps.

The mob was by now out of control, and what happened next turned the riot into an insurrection. In front of the law courts were displayed the wooden panels on which official portraits of the imperial family were painted. These portraits partook of the sacred character which attached to the imperial office; indeed the painted representation of the emperor at a law court signified that, as the personification of the law itself, the sovereign was present in all the imperial courts throughout the empire, and legal decisions were made in his name. But it was the Emperor against whom the mob's anger was directed. Some people in the crowd picked up stones and hurled them at the portraits, and it was not long before the panels began to split and shatter.

Nothing like this had ever happened in Antioch before. This was *laesa maiestas*, the equivalent, actually, of stoning the Emperor himself, for the Emperor's power resided in the portrait, and what was done to the effigy was considered as being done to his sacred person.

Having done this much, the mob did not stop, but went on to attack the bronze statues of Theodosius, his wife, and the prince Arcadius which stood in the square. Ropes were attached to the statues and they were pulled from the bases and dragged about. Arms and heads broke off and were kicked about on the stone pavement.

At this point the authorities dispatched messengers to Constantinople with news of the rebellion. A house was set on fire and the mob began to grow and spread. But now the course of the rebellion began to change. The archers who served as police arrived and began to put out the fire, and the Count of the East appeared with his military guard and began to arrest the rioters. It was by now midday, and order began to be restored.

It was long before people in Antioch forgot what happened then. Once the authorities were in control of the situation, they acted with the greatest speed and—in keeping with the contemporary conception of justice—brutality. Trials were conducted swiftly, and according to the degree of their guilt the prisoners were beheaded, burned alive, or reserved to be eaten alive by wild animals in the arena. Exceptions were not made for children, and some were burned alive.

When the people had recovered their senses a little, they began to imagine what punishments the Emperor might decide to inflict on the city. In keeping with the imperial practice on such occasions, the city might be punished as a whole. Rumors began to go about—with as much basis as rumors usually have. The troops were to be permitted to loot and devastate the city. All the senators were to be executed. Private property was to be confiscated. A hush fell on the whole city; the feeling of apprehension was palpable.

As the Bishop and the clergy watched the riot, they realized what this would mean, when the disorders were at an end, for the people under their care. It would have been impossible for anyone to stop the riot; but when the mob had scattered, it was the turn of the Bishop and his priests to minister to their people. Bishop Flavian knew no more than anyone else what might happen; but it was clear that all the citizens of Antioch, pagan as well as Christian, were in need of comfort and counsel. Here indeed was an occasion for teaching the terrified people the difference between insecurity and real security.

The Bishop determined to set off for Constantinople at once, to intercede with the Emperor; and before he left, he selected John Chrysostom, as the most eloquent of his priests, and bade him preach in the Old Church a series of sermons on the disaster.

The twenty-one sermons *On the Statues* were preached during Lent. The city by this time was thoroughly subdued. Imperial commissioners had arrived from Constantinople and had begun an investigation, on the basis of which they would make a report and a recommendation to the Emperor. They brought with them an imperial decree in which a preliminary punishment was ordained. The city was deprived of its title of metropolis—by this period a merely titular rank, though still highly prized—and was made subordinate, administratively, to its ancient rival Laodicea-on-the-Sea, a much smaller and less important place than Antioch. The baths, the theatres, and the hippodromes were all closed—a sore punishment for people such as the Antiochenes—and the daily distribution of free bread to the poor of the city was suspended.

As was customary on such occasions, the senators of Antioch were held responsible for the riot, and it was the task of the imperial commissioners to determine the degree of their guilt. Some years previously Libanius, as the leading citizen of Antioch, had been given the honorary rank of praetorian prefect, and in virtue of this he sat with the commissioners during the inquiry. A silent crowd gathered in the street outside the commissioners' headquarters while the hearings were being held. John Chrysostom at first stood among the hushed people in the street, then made his way into the courtyard of the building, in which it was possible to hear the proceedings inside.

Every day John Chrysostom attended the hearings, and every day he preached his sermon in the Old Church. The commissioners were proving themselves just, though very firm; but the city was still filled with foreboding, for it was announced that the senators were to be imprisoned until the Emperor's decision was brought from Constantinople. Chrysostom watched the melancholy spectacle of the senators being led in chains across the market place to a building next to the council-chamber, where they were to be confined.

Citizens who had to watch such sights were very ready

to listen to what their famous preacher had to say, and Chrysostom realized that here an opportunity was given him. He reminded the people of their sins of covetousness and pride which had caused the riot, though the leading part in the disorder he attributed to strangers who had come into Antioch from other places—and in this he was probably right. In their terror, they must recall that their safety lay with God, their loving Father. They must show fortitude and patience, and they must refrain from making foolish vows as they sought to obtain deliverance. Fear of magistrates was a beneficial thing, enjoined by the New Testament. Grief and repentance would cure sin. God the creator by his act of creation showed his love for men, and it would be possible for the people to restore their true relationship with God.

When John Chrysostom was midway in his course of sermons, word came from Constantinople that the Emperor, at the intercession of the Bishop, and on the basis of the commissioners' report, taken by fast messenger to the capital, had been graciously pleased to pardon the city and remove all the penalties that had been imposed on it. The rejoicing was tremendous; but Chrysostom did not put an end to his discourses. Now he could point out how grateful to God the people should be for their deliverance, and remind them how salutary their fear and repentance had been. In all these discourses Chrysostom took full advantage of its being the Lenten season to point out the importance of fasting and self-examination.

The news of the imperial pardon reached Antioch about Palm Sunday, and during the following week the Bishop himself returned, having traveled the long journey from Constantinople at top speed in spite of his age. To the joy of the Easter season the city could now add special rejoicing. The festival Easter service at which the Bishop presided was joyful and magnificent even beyond its usual splendor. Houses were illuminated and public banquets were held in the streets. Many pagans had been so impressed by the demeanor of the Christians and by the behavior of the Bishop and his clergy that they were converted to Christianity.

For the Christian leaders of the city, there was actually much more involved than just a riot. The riot of course was a unique explosion of disorder; but to the Christian thinker it could, like everything else in life, be turned to some good. As Chrysostom thought of the episode and sought to know what it really meant, he thought he understood that what was really involved was a question of Christian citizenship. One of the pastor's most important functions was to lead his people to see what the true nature of their Christian calling was. From this dreadful morning of disorder, people might learn something of man's dual role. He was created in the image of God, and he always represented that image, however much it might be defaced or obscured by sin. Man's true citizenship was in heaven, in the heavenly Jerusalem, the city of the living God. Here on earth Christians had no permanent home, but were seekers after the city which was to come.

It was true that for his people God's call was everything. But this riot drove home the truth that so long as he was on earth and a member of a mundane community the Christian was inescapably a citizen of the empire, and specifically —in the case of Chrysostom's people—of the city of Antioch. This was an earthly citizenship that the Christian could not escape so long as he was living in the midst of his fellow men. Antioch, it was all too plain, was a pagan city; but it was also a Christian city of the first rank in the history of the faith.

Here indeed was a lesson of which the Christians of Antioch needed to be reminded. Christianity, unlike any of the pagan cults, was a historical religion, in which divine truth had been revealed in historical events. Through the past, God was still revealing himself to the present. This was one of the essential differences of Christianity from paganism. In this context, the city of Antioch was a special witness to the faith, and the Christians of successive generations who lived there must be worthy witness to the history of the city. "Our city," the preacher declared in his third homily, "is dearer to Christ than all other cities, both because of the virtue of our ancestors, and of your own virtues." Thus the Christians of Antioch must live as a part of the great tradition, and so the city would be dear to Christ.

As a pupil of Libanius, Chrysostom was well aware of the classical doctrine of the city as the center of civilization, the city built up by the virtues and good will of its citizens. Libanius had tried to teach his pupils the virtues of the citizen of the polis. Chrysostom knew the Antioch which lived in the mind of his pagan teacher, and he had perforce, as he sat under Libanius, heard of the classical virtues which went to mold the ideal dweller in the polis. But there were Christian virtues as well, and it was out of these that the true Christian should be formed as he lived in the earthly community of his fellows. The Christian community, in its corporate act of witness and worship, was made up of individuals, and the link between the faith of the individual and the witness of the community was essential. If Libanius taught that the polis depended upon the virtues of its people, the idea of the Christian and his relation to his polis had changed totally because Christianity brought an entirely new concept of man and his nature.

This new man, this "new creation," lived in an ancient polis, but he was called to live in it differently. As a result the polis itself would be a new creation. Chrysostom spoke eloquently of this new Antioch in his seventeenth sermon:

Do you grieve that the dignity of the city is taken away? Learn what the dignity of a city is; and then you will know clearly that if the inhabitants do not betray it, no one else will be able to take away the dignity of a city. Not the fact that it is a metropolis; nor that it contains large and beautiful buildings; nor that it has many columns and spacious porticoes and walks, nor that it is named in proclamations before other cities, but the virtue and piety of its inhabitants; this is a city's dignity and ornament and defense; since if these things are not found in it, it is the most insignificant in the world, though it may enjoy unlimited honor from Emperors!

This was not a unique idea on Chrysostom's part. His younger contemporary Nemesius, the scholarly bishop of Emesa, not far from Antioch, wrote in his learned treatise *On the Nature of Man* on the significance of the city for the human race and society, adapting Platonic doctrine to Christian thought:

Because of the arts and sciences and the useful things to which they lead, we have mutual need of one another. And because we need one another, we come together into one place in large numbers, and share with each other the necessities of our life, in common intercourse. To this human assemblage and cohabitation we have given the name of city. And therein we have profit from one another, by propinquity, and by not needing to travel. For man is a naturally sociable animal, and made for citizenship. No single person is in all ways self-sufficient. And so it is clear, how that cities exist for the sake of intercourse, and for the sake of learning from each other.

The Christian community was founded upon *agapé*, love —an idea strange to pagan thinkers, who had got as far as the idea of righteousness as the basis of human social and political activity, but had never been able to envisage love in this connection. Christian ascetic thinkers, notably Chrysostom's older contemporary Basil of Caesarea, had been contemplating the nature of the monastic community, into which the Christian seeker retired in order, by freeing himself from the desires of the flesh and the trammels of the world, to seek the nature of God and place himself in surer touch with ultimate reality than he could in the world. These new communities, in the nature of human relationships, presented the same situations as the city, for their practical success as social groups depended upon harmony and virtue. Thus the essential element in the monastic community was *agapê*, love.

To some Christians, the monastic community, as the ideal form of human life, might seem to be the Christian successor to the pagan polis. But Chrysostom and Bishop Nemesius of Emesa thought differently. The riot at Antioch showed what was at stake. It was as Roman citizens, living in Antioch, the capital of the province of Syria and of the Diocese of the East, that the Christian people of the city had to bear witness. If Antioch was still a partly pagan, partly Christian city, it would someday, according to the divine plan, be a wholly Christian city, and the riot might be a signpost to point to what the city must be. Libanius had thought that the old polis was threatened, and he linked the decline of his world with the decline of polis. From his point of view this was true; but Libanius did not realize that the Christians were able to think of a new kind of polis with a new kind of citizenship based on love. Thus in new terms the old and fruitful idea of the polis was to continue to fulfill itself. It was one of the tasks of the bishop of Antioch and his clergy, John Chrysostom among them, to guide this fulfillment.

CHAPTER VII

THE HOLY MYSTERIES

"Taste ye of the fountain of immortal life."

—DIVINE LITURGY ATTRIBUTED TO ST. JOHN CHRYSOSTOM

A S he walked about the streets of the city, the visitor would see that many of the private houses and shops which belonged to Christians had religious inscriptions carved on them, often on the stone frames of the doors and windows. To anyone who had lived or traveled in the Greek Christian East, such inscriptions were familiar, attesting as they did the Christian consciousness that all life was lived within the framework of God's gifts and God's protection.

One of the commonest formulas on lintels was the declaration of the Christian faith: *There is one God only*. Another text would read: *Our Lord Jesus Christ, the Son, the Word of God, dwells here: let no evil enter*. Another inscription, accompanied by small disks containing the cross, read: *Where the cross is present, the enemy shall not prevail*. A similar text, accompanied by crosses, guarded another house: *Of this house the Lord shall guard the entrance and the exit; for the cross being set before, no malignant eye shall prevail against it*. In spite of Christian teaching, the belief in the evil eye had not wholly disappeared. Another lintel contained a disk inscribed with the cross in relief, and the words *I am set for the peace of those that dwell here*.

There were numerous phrases appealing for the Lord's help. A very common one was the quotation from the Psalms, inscribed over doors: *The Lord shall guard thy coming in and thy going out, from now even for evermore, amen.* In another house, the dwellers were protected by the words *Jesus of Nazareth, who was born of Mary, the Son of God, dwells here.* On another lintel was inscribed *The power of God and Christ erected this house,* followed by the date. A large house bore phrases from a Psalm: *Thou hast put gladness in my heart. From the harvest of grain and wine and oil were we filled in peace.* Elsewhere one might see the well-known words *The Lord is my shepherd, and nothing shall I want.*

Several houses bore over their doors the words *If God be for us who is against us?* Another inscription consisted of the prayer *Lord, help this house, and those that dwell in it.* Over another door was written: *The Lord of hosts is with us, the God of Jacob is our defender.* A large house had the first two verses of the Ninety-first Psalm inscribed over its door: *He that dwelleth in the help of the Most High . . .* Another Psalm was quoted on a lintel: *Let thy mercy, Lord, be upon us, according as we hoped in thee.*

Such inscriptions were common throughout the city, on houses of all kinds, from the mansions of the wealthy to the smallest and poorest dwellings. Here and there among them one would see a pagan inscription, the words addressed directly to the reader: *What thou sayest, friend, may that be to thee also, twofold,* or *If thou blessest this house and its inmates may thy blessings return upon thee, and if thou cursest, may thy curses return upon thee, doubled.*

The Christian inscriptions were the open expression, in a world still partly pagan, of a deep and pervasive piety. Individually they were witness to the desire of their owners to try to remember God in all their activities. Likewise, both in their phrases from the Bible and in their prayers, these inscriptions reminded all who saw them of the great corporate act of thanksgiving and worship, the Eucharist, which was the primary public expression of the faith. A Christian visitor to Antioch would be eager to attend a celebration of the Eucharist in the Great Church, where the rite was surrounded with all the magnificence fitted to this service in the city in which the followers had first been called Christians.

While the Eucharist—sometimes called the Divine Liturgy —was the essential and most important service of worship in the church, it was not something that had come into being fully developed and in final form. Originally it had been a commemoration of the Last Supper, in which the Lord symbolically offered to his followers his Body, which was given for them, and his Blood of the New Covenant, which was shed for the remission of their sins. This act of communion the Lord commanded them to repeat in his memory. As time passed the rite had naturally and inevitably developed into a gathering for worship that for the average Christian, not thinking in terms of formal theology, came to represent a memorial of the incarnation and life of Christ and his death and resurrection, and an encounter of the Lord and his people, in which the faithful had an opportunity, through partaking of the sacred elements, of coming into communion with the Lord.

What was represented was the self-revelation of God in Christ, and the continued offering to humanity of his revelation, through which the believer could find himself in immediate touch with the source of salvation. The liturgical repetition of the act of communion afforded the believer the opportunity to go forward in an increasingly deepened understanding of the nature of Christ and of God. The fellowship in which this communion was realized served to give added strength and authority to the experience received by the individual. The Eucharist did not take the place of private prayer, but strengthened it.

In this experience the individual perceived and understood in true perspective both his own nature as creature and the nature of God as Creator. The Eucharistic rite brought out the response of the creature to the Creator, the response of the human soul to the goodness of God; and in the moment of receiving the Body and the Blood the communicant could realize a bond that would give him strength for his life of obedience. It was to embody and manifest this experience that the Divine Liturgy had been developed; and it was to express this experience in the most perfect form possible that the bishops continued to strive to improve the literary form of the service. The service had grown by accretion and improvement, each section taking its place as an indispensable part of the whole.

Of course every individual who attended the Divine Liturgy did so with his own spiritual history behind him, and the act of communion could not but have a particular significance for each communicant—just as successive communions might each have a special significance for an individual communicant. There were all degrees of personal piety and devotion in each Christian community, and all stages of progress in the Christian life. The many communicants who were illiterate approached the Body and Blood with their own devotion, just as the highly educated imperial functionaries and senators brought to the communion their background of philosophical training. The bishops, priests, and deacons came to the rite with their own spiritual theology, issuing in mystical experience. Yet it was the same Body and Blood that drew them all, and the same Savior to whom they all looked. The eternal life that was offered was a reality to them all. If it had not been, the Divine Liturgy would have ceased to be celebrated.

For the bishop or priest who officiated at the Eucharist, it was an awesome duty and privilege. He was in fact to invoke the descent of the Holy Spirit on the bread and wine, and he was to touch with his hands, and administer to his people, the Body and Blood of the Savior. John Chrysostom in his treatise *On the Priesthood* described the great place occupied by the celebration of the Eucharist in the function of the priest, and the sense of spiritual terror which the celebrant's act might inspire:

> The priestly office is indeed discharged on earth, but it ranks among heavenly ordinances; and very naturally so, for neither man, nor angel, nor archangel, nor any other created power, but the Comforter Himself instituted this vocation, and persuaded men while still abiding in the flesh to represent the ministry of angels. Wherefore the consecrated priest ought to be as pure as if he were standing in the heavens themselves in the midst of those powers. Fearful, indeed, and of most awful import, were the things which were used before the dispensation of grace, such as the bells, the pomegranates, the stones on the breastplate and on the richly embroidered garment, the girdle, the mitre, the long robe, the plate of gold, the holy of holies, the deep silence within [cf. Exodus 28:4 ff.]. But if anyone should examine the things which belong to the dispensation of grace, he will find that, small as they are, yet they are fearful and full of awe, and that what was spoken concerning the law is true in this case also, that "the splendor that once was is now no splendor at all; it is outshone by a splendor greater still [2 Cor. 3:10]." For when you see the Lord sacrificed, and laid upon the altar, and the priest standing and praying over the victim, and all the worshipers empurpled with that precious blood, can you then think that you are still

among men, and standing upon the earth? Are you not, on the contrary, straightway translated to Heaven, and casting out every carnal thought from the soul, do you not with disembodied spirit and pure reason contemplate the things which are in Heaven? Oh, what a marvel! What love of God to man! He who sits on high with the Father is at that hour held in the hands of all, and gives Himself to those who are willing to embrace and grasp Him. And this all do through the eyes of faith! Do these things seem to you fit to be despised, or such as to make it possible for anyone to be uplifted against them?

Would you also learn from another miracle the exceeding sanctity of this office? Picture Elijah and the vast multitude standing around him [cf. 1 Kings 18], and the sacrifice laid upon the altar of stones, and all the rest of the people hushed into a deep silence while the prophet alone offers up prayer: then the sudden rush of fire from Heaven upon the sacrifice. These are marvelous things, charged with terror. Now then pass from this scene to the rites which are celebrated in the present day. They are not only marvelous to behold, but transcendent in terror. There stands the priest, not bringing down fire from Heaven, but the Holy Spirit. He makes prolonged supplication, not that some flame sent down from on high may consume the offerings, but that grace descending on the sacrifice may thereby enlighten the souls of all, and render them more refulgent than silver purified by fire. Who can despise this most awful mystery, unless he is stark mad and senseless? Or do you not know that no human soul could have endured that fire in the sacrifice, but all would have been utterly consumed, had not the assistance of God's grace been great?

For if anyone will consider how great a thing it is for one, being a man, and compassed with flesh and blood, to be enabled to draw nigh to that blessed and pure nature, he will then clearly see what great honor the grace of the Spirit has vouchsafed to priests, since by their agency these rites are celebrated, and others nowise inferior to these both in respect to our dignity and our salvation. For they who inhabit the earth and make their abode there are entrusted with the administration of things which are in Heaven, and have received an authority which God has not given to angels or archangels.

It is not surprising that some men, perhaps overly sensitive, resisted ordination, fearing its awful responsibilities, even though their superiors thought them worthy.

In every church, the Eucharist was celebrated every Sunday and every saint's day; and in the cathedrals and in the largest churches, as well as in religious communities, it was celebrated daily. Depending upon the length of the sermon (or sermons, for there were sometimes more than one), the whole celebration, including the preparatory services, would last between two and three hours.

The first part of the service consisted of the Mass of the catechumens, as persons undergoing instruction preparatory to baptism were called. The service opened with the salutation from the celebrant, "Peace be with you," to which the congregation responded, "and with thy spirit." After prayers, lessons were read from the prophets of the Old Testament and from the Epistles (or the Acts of the Apostles) and the Gospel. The selections to be read were prescribed in a lectionary, so that the reading on a particular day might be especially suitable to the significance of that day, if it were a saint's day or the commemoration of an event in the life of Christ. The salutation was repeated, and the sermon was preached. On occasion several sermons would be delivered, by the bishop and one or more of the priests, or by several of the priests, if no bishop were present.

At the close of the sermon came the dismissal of the various kinds of people who were not permitted to remain throughout the Eucharist since they were not fitted to receive the

consecrated elements, namely the catechumens and the penitents who were undergoing discipline for infractions of
church order or for confessed sins, and had to remain for a
certain amount of time, prescribed by the bishop or priest,
without receiving the sacrament. Prayers were offered for
each class as they were dismissed in turn, with the deacon
supervising the withdrawal.

When the catechumens and the penitents had departed,
the doors of the church, opened up to this point, were closed,
so that no unauthorized person might see or hear the Eucharist proper, which followed. To begin, the deacon, with
the words "Let us pray," opened the litany of intercessory
prayers.

It was here that the universal character of the Eucharist
was declared. Prayers were said for the peace of the whole
world, and for the stability and prosperity of the churches
of God. After this there was a prayer for the bishops and
clergy, and this was followed by one for kings and rulers.
There followed prayers for the sick, for those who had been
condemned to hard labor in mines (a usual punishment at
that time for serious crimes), and for those possessed of evil
spirits. Prayers for travelers by land or sea, and for good
weather, followed; and the litany ended with a petition for
the sending of "the angel of peace," and a prayer that all
the undertakings of the congregation might be directed toward peaceful purposes. At the close of the litany the officiant and the congregation again saluted one another, and then
the officiant blessed the congregation.

After anthems and psalms, the offering of the elements,
the bread and the wine, began. Again there was the salutation of the congregation and the response. This was followed
by the thanksgiving:

Priest: *Let us give thanks unto the Lord.*

Response: *It is meet and right so to worship the Father, the Son, and the Holy Spirit, the Trinity consubstantial and undivided.*

This was followed by the singing of the Trisagion (Thrice-Holy) hymn:

Holy, holy, holy, Lord of Sabaoth, heaven and earth are full of thy glory. Hosanna in the highest; blessed is he that cometh in the name of the Lord; Hosanna in the highest.

Of this thanksgiving, Chrysostom wrote in one of his sermons:

We rehearse over the cup the ineffable blessings of God and whatever benefits we enjoy; and so we offer it and communicate, giving Him thanks that He hath delivered mankind from error; that when we were afar off He hath made us near; that when we had no hope and were without God He hath made us brethren and fellow heirs with Himself. For these and all the like blessings we give Him thanks and so draw nigh.

It was at this point that the celebrant, the bread and wine having been placed on the altar, recited the words with which the Lord instituted the communion. As he rehearsed the events of the Last Supper, the bishop or priest at the appropriate moment spoke the words of Jesus as He distributed the bread and wine:

Take, eat. This is my body which is broken for you, for the remission of sins. Drink ye all of this. This is my blood of the New Covenant, which is shed for you and for many for the remission of sins.

This was followed by the prayer in which God was invoked to send down His Holy Spirit so that it might "come and touch" the sacred gifts, the bread and wine, lying on the altar.

At this moment it was considered particularly efficacious to offer prayers for the departed, at the time when "the common Sacrifice of the world is before us." The celebrant then recited prayers for the dead, including martyrs, confessors, and priests. Those of the congregation who wished could give the clergy, before the service, the names of deceased relatives and friends whose names they desired to have mentioned.

The celebrant then broke the bread, and further intercessory prayers were said. The time of the actual communion was approaching. After the bishops, priests, and deacons had received the elements (administered by the bishop or the chief officiant), the remainder of the congregation came forward—subdeacons, readers (a minor order of clergy who read the lessons and psalms), singers, ascetics, deaconnesses, unmarried women, widows, children, and the remainder of the laity in order of rank. Women received the communion wearing veils.

As the bishop or priest administered the sacred elements to each individual he spoke the words "The Body of Christ . . . The Blood of Christ, the cup of life." While the communion was taking place, Psalm 34, containing the words "O taste and see how gracious the Lord is," was sung.

When all had communicated, the remains of the bread and wine which had not been consumed were carried away by the deacons. The bishop or officiating priest then said a prayer of thanksgiving for the communion, and the people were dismissed.

Such, in outline, was the service of the Eucharist. The beauty of the anthems and the prayers, mingled with the clouds of incense, the gorgeous vestments of the priests, and the colorful decorations of the churches, made the service an offering of praise and thanksgiving worthy of the Ruler of the Universe. In a large church, such as the Great Church at Antioch, the communion vessels would be of gold, ornamented with precious stones, presented by the emperor himself. The physical splendor of the rite was not designed for mere display. It was felt that God manifested himself in all creation and in all the physical beauty of the material world, and that Christ the King should be worshiped and glorified in a manner worthy of a sovereign ruler who had created the world and given its riches to mankind. The splendor of the ceremony was devised in conscious appreciation of the beauty of creation in which God's goodness is revealed. The lighted candles and lamps, burning in daylight, were a sign of joy.

As the faithful united to worship God and to come into communion with him, they also united in communion with one another, and with their fellows throughout the church; and they were especially aware that this communion included not only the Christians who were on the earth at that moment, but all those who had gone before, as well as all Christians who would follow them in the future. This fellowship of the whole communion of saints, all sharing in the redemptive work of Christ, was a theme that ran through the whole of the Eucharist. As he participated in this service, the Christian was one member, along with the rest, in a community, counting neither more nor less than each other member—so that in this sense the Christian loved his neighbor as himself.

The service constituted in fact a literary and ceremonial vehicle through which divine truth and divine reality would be communicable to men. The Divine Liturgy was a visible invocation and communication of the motive force behind the lives of Christians. As the embodiment of the relationship between God and man, the act of communion conveyed redemption and salvation. Reflecting the experience of Christians of the past, it offered the substance of the faith to those of the present and the assurance that believers in future years would find the same source in man's response to divine love. The Eucharist provided the moment for self-realization both for the individual and for the community.

The Divine Liturgy was not only a corporate act of worship and of communion. It was also a public declaration of allegiance to the faith and a manifestation of solidarity to the outside world. If it was the center of spiritual life of the community as well as of the individual, it was likewise the central symbol of the distinction between Christians and pagans. To the Christian, the Eucharist represented the continuity of the church as an institution as well as the central place which the church occupied in human life in general and in the life of the community in particular. Possessing the Eucharist, commemorating the source of man's salvation taking place within the community, the Christian more than ever looked upon the pagan as attempting to live independently of God—living in "a world without hope and without God." The Eucharist as a source of power and renewal was incomprehensible to pagans who had no equivalent rite which was available to the whole pagan community.

Libanius' father—the fathers of Libanius' friends and contemporaries—remembered Antioch in the days before the conversion to Christianity of the Emperor Constantine. They had known of, and possibly had witnessed, the martyrdoms of the Christians who perished in the persecution under Diocletian. The Bishop of Antioch, Cyril, was condemned to hard labor in the government-owned marble quarries in Pannonia, a sentence that in the case of a person such as a bishop was calculated to mean slow death from starvation, exposure, and maltreatment. A characteristic episode was the martyrdom of Romanus, a deacon who through his life and death became one of the principal saints of Antioch. He was condemned to be burned at the stake, by the Roman method according to which a pit was dug and the victim was buried up to his knees so that the flames might reach him more quickly. The Caesar Galerius, who happened to be in the city at the time, stopped the execution, but ordered instead the prisoner's tongue to be cut out, an operation that usually resulted in the victim's dying of shock and loss of blood. Romanus lived, but was later executed in prison.

Such stories as these were still told in Antioch in the days of Theodosius. How the fortune of the church had changed since then! Outwardly the city of Antioch had not altered very greatly since the time of Diocletian and Constantine. In dress and in their occupations the people of the city, to an outside observer, would not have looked essentially different. The city was still a busy commercial center, provincial capital, and military headquarters. But in the churches and in their celebrations of the Eucharist a great change was symbolized. It was true that the life of the city was not yet wholly transformed. But John Chrysostom and the other priests of Antioch hoped that their people like a leaven would gradually affect the lump.

CHAPTER VIII

OLD AND NEW: PAST AND FUTURE

"Hold fast the traditions."

—II THESSALONIANS

IF people in Antioch had been inclined to look ahead, would they have seen anything in the Antioch of the reign of Theodosius the Great that would surprise the future? If a citizen of the modern world, considering this idea, could by some magical means be transported back to the Antioch of the time of Theodosius the Great, he would have a number of questions to ask of Libanius and John Chrysostom. Knowing, himself, what the course of ancient history had been, the supernatural visitor would among other things be curious to know what Libanius and John Chrysostom during their lifetime expected of the future. Modern men are concerned for the future, and curious about it. Thus the visitor might be surprised to find that Libanius and John Chrysostom did not seem as much interested in his question as he was.

In reality, this would not have been because men in antiquity were not concerned with the future, but because these two particular men were not thinking very much about it. Their attitude, the visitor would come to realize, was significant for the time and the place, and for these men and their friends whom they represented.

Libanius had been brought up in terms of the past and of

146

the meaning of the past for the present. But in his world, the significance of the continuity of the past and the present had been threatened, if not actually affected, by the intrusion of "the Galilean madness"—Christianity. Libanius would very likely try hard to mask his feeling from the strange visitor, as he did, probably, from his own contemporaries—even, indeed, from himself; but it must have seemed plain to anyone that a man like Libanius could not—from his own point of view—have expected very much from the future. Libanius had witnessed the failure of his friend the Emperor Julian to revive the old religion, and by the time of Theodosius' reign, twenty years or more later, anyone would suppose that the most that Libanius could hope for was that something at least of Hellenism might be salvaged and preserved. One could no longer hope for recovery or revival. Survival of a part of the tradition was perhaps the most that one could desire. At least Libanius faced the future with real courage.

To a man like John Chrysostom, the future was a totally different thing. To him the future was assured because it meant the coming in due time of the Kingdom of God on earth. The Kingdom must come, and the future was the preparation for its coming. True, the coming would doubtless not be immediate, and the servants of God must do their share in preparation for it. The servants of God such as John Chrysostom must in fact be prepared to encounter obstacles in the way of their labors. But the outcome itself could not be in doubt. John Chrysostom did not, like Libanius, have to hide his feelings. The future of his own life was something to be looked on with joy and confidence, and the future of Antioch—and of the world—after his own departure would only be an assured progress toward the consummation of all things in Christ.

Such might be the expectancies of men who personified

the two religious traditions which had come to form the Antioch of the time of Theodosius. If the visitor, having conversed with Libanius and John Chrysostom, were to turn with his question to less eminent persons—or perhaps one should say persons less closely and less keenly concerned with religious traditions, and less introspective about the future— he might gain yet another insight into the expectations of the men of that world.

If, for example, he were to take his question to a member of the imperial administration, such as the Count of the East or the governor of Syria, he might find still another point of view. To such officers, there could be no doubt, of course, that the future was secure and assured. Was not the eternity of the Roman Empire one of the oldest political axioms? The times might be troubled, the power of the Persians and the barbarians might have become a constant factor in the thoughts of every emperor and his advisers, there might be economic and social difficulties at home; but the empire had endured for many centuries, and had always survived its problems and its crises. The new shape the state had been taking during the past hundred years seemed better fitted than ever to carry on the history of the Roman people.

In their own day, these officials could see, the state was becoming more and more what a Christian Roman Emperor would wish it to be. The devout and serious Theodosius had been able to take a step that had not been possible for the great Constantine; he had issued imperial legislation enforcing orthodoxy by law and making religious error subject not only to divine wrath but to action of the secular arm. Legislation against pagan practices was intensified. Surely the church was in a happy state, even though paganism was not wholly dead and even though the Arian error, at last

nothing but an insignificant town under the domination of Islam, a religion never dreamed of by either Theodosius or Justinian.

The future would come, and no one could say what it might bring. The important thing, to Libanius and John Chrysostom and their peers, was to maintain the traditions—to hand on to the future the noble accomplishment of the past, so that the future might enjoy the achievement which had been given to the world. The strength of mankind and (whether for Christian or pagan) the salvation of mankind were rooted in the past, as the past expressed itself and made itself effective in the present. If Libanius and John Chrysostom had been able to foresee that one day Antioch as they knew it would cease to exist, and that the bearer of the tradition would be Constantinople, that would have been a blow, of course, to a lover of Antioch; but even so the important thing would be the ongoing life of the tradition.

People in Antioch, of whatever religious allegiance or intellectual background, were grateful to the past—that is, to the particular past to which they themselves looked back—out of which they knew they had been formed. Every educated man of that time, with any experience of practical affairs, believed in the significance and the implications of his own roots in the past. Indeed a man who was not conscious of this debt would seem not only ungrateful but ignorant. Such a man would be unable to understand the present.

Within this framework, the future was clearly understood to be not simply a chronological sequence following present time but a development out of the present, which itself represented the unbroken thread of the past. Thus in this continuous process of history, while the future might bring some accidental development which might be unforeseen, it would still be shaped and conditioned to at least some extent by its antecedents. In the belief of the church, the Christians of the present were linked not only with the Christians of the past, but with those who would be Christians in the future. This assurance was matched by the traditional belief in the eternity of the Roman Empire. These two tenets provided a basis for confidence which in effect meant that essentially the future might be looked upon as under the control of the present. Religious, social, and intellectual life—one whole—was thus made up of elements which represented an established, continuous, and ongoing tradition. The responsibility for custody and preservation of something that had been tried and proved was an essential part of the tradition; and this tradition had found its physical manifestation in the life of the polis.

Thus such a historical development as the fall of Antioch and the transfer of the substance of the culture to Constantinople was an incident, not necessarily a check. In the process of transfer Constantinople would naturally add its own contribution; but the important element in the culture was the substance, not the location; and the culture while it grew up in a city was not necessarily attached to one city. Athens had declined physically, but its civilization had been diffused through the world, and some of it remained in Athens itself. A man was inevitably attached to his city, and the city had an indispensable role in the formation and transmission of civilization, but the civilization really existed in people, not in buildings—though the people had created these buildings as an expression of their civilization. What Libanius was attached to was the people in their environment, and to him the environment was an essential factor. Christianity recognized and appreciated the environment, but it was more interested in people, specifically as individuals, and people were in Christianity no longer primarily the citizens of a polis, as they had been to pre-Christian students of the social organism, such as Plato and Aristotle. They were now members of the Body of Christ, a concept which overrode all other social ideas and ideals.

But it was in cities which had come into being as ancient classical *poleis* that Christians for the most part had to live. Constantinople was the only great city of the empire planned from the beginning as a Christian city, and even so it had the outward forms of a classical polis, simply because no other kind of a city was conceivable to the founders and designers of cities. The foundation of Constantinople as a new Christian imperial capital was a recognition that the polis could take on a new spirit, the Christian spirit, and that the Holy Spirit could work in the lives of men as well within the environment of a classical polis as it could anywhere else. Classical civilization had consciously centered itself in the city, while Christianity centered itself in the household of God, the Christian community; and if Christian culture found that it was possible to absorb classical culture within itself, then the city ceased to be an end and became a means.

Here a city like Antioch would be transformed in the process by which it passed from a classical polis to a Christian community. It remained the city of Antioch, capital of Syria, seat of the Count of the East, "Fair Crown of the Orient"; but it was now a different city. This was a change such as Libanius could not understand, because nothing in his training or his environment had prepared his mind for it. John Chrysostom, being primarily a pastor, was more intent upon the immediate needs of his people than upon the eventual development of their environment. He knew that every generation of Christians had to be converted afresh. If he had been disposed to look into the future, he would have approved; but it was not to the future development of the city of Antioch that he would have looked ahead. What he looked toward was the coming of the Kingdom.

Libanius and Chrysostom summed up in themselves all that had gone to make up the Antioch of their time. Not only that, but their personal relationship was significant. Chrysostom had been the pupil of Libanius, and according to the local tradition had been considered by Libanius to be his most brilliant pupil. To this extent the new depended upon the old. But according to the same tradition, Libanius on his deathbed refused to allow his famous Christian pupil to be named as his successor at the head of his school. Thus the old and the new were ultimately incompatible.

Yet these two men had one important thought in common. Both thought of the past as being involved in the present— but the implications were different and the significance of the past for the future was different. Libanius' world, rooted in a past composed of many elements, only expected, or hoped, to maintain itself; its future was perforce a closed and limited vision. Chrysostom's world was also rooted in the past, but this was a past centered about a historical event—"under Pontius Pilate"—which was the beginning of other events. The future would be the certainty of a continual ascent toward something better, until all things were consummated. The Christian past would simply grow and develop itself.

Can we see, in all this, what it was that kept some pagans forever apart from Christianity? Libanius' point of view may suggest the reason, or one of the reasons, why men like Libanius and Themistius, and even Julian, who had once nominally been a Christian, were unable either to understand the Christian point of view or to appreciate the strength of Christianity and the reasons for its present success, as well as its certain prospect of continued expansion. The emancipation of Christianity and the social and political developments of the fourth century forced men, both pagans and Christians, to think anew about the meaning of the world and about the significance of man and of his life in the world. The Christian answer, in the hands of the great series of theologians the fourth century produced, took into account not only Christian doctrine as such, but the classical respect for antiquity and for the achievements of the great men of the past which was one of the essentials of the classical tradition. This point of view was applied even to theology; for example, Basil the Great in his treatise *On the Holy Spirit* declared that the theologians of sound character "hold the dignity of antiquity [i.e., of the ancient church] to be more honorable than mere new-fangled novelty" and that such men would "preserve the traditions of their fathers unadulterated." To the Christians, the truth would prove itself.

This was how the Christians could solve their problems. What of the pagans? When they were challenged to discern and affirm what it was that they were living for, they could only fall back upon their literary traditions into which nothing new might be admitted because the truth of the traditions had been demonstrated by their antiquity and their durability. If Christianity seemed to tend to discredit these traditions, then Christianity must be wrong. Themistius and Julian knew something about Christian teaching, but whatever they knew was not, to them, adequate to displace the intellectual heritage of the classical past. One cardinal element of this heritage was the polis as a center of civilization, and to Libanius this was still the core about which the true life of mankind should properly be built. To Libanius no other frame of reference was possible. Christians like his pupil John Chrysostom might speak in terms of the polis, but to Libanius a Christian polis could have no meaning.

Christians and pagans each held one truth. The Christian truth, being universal, could be opened up, so to speak, and expanded to receive any belief or idea which could prove itself to be a part of the larger truth; this of course was how some aspects of Greek thought were absorbed in the new Christian civilization. To the pagans, any such fresh and continuing realization of the truth was simply not possible; indeed it was unnecessary. To Libanius and his peers, the new system the Christians had introduced as the reason of life was not acceptable—not even comprehensible—because it would not agree with the truth of antiquity. So it was that to Libanius the world was declining and could do nothing else but decline, with real civilization surviving only in what was left of the polis, while to the Christians the new life and the new culture, less sensitive to the decline and decay the pagans felt, could take the polis for granted and build on it.

Today's students may be apt to think in modern terms of the conflict between paganism and Christianity. The term "paganism" indeed has taken on special connotations through its use with reference to Christianity and in the light of the outcome of the contest. Libanius and his peers did not think in these terms. What in later times was thought of as "paganism" was to Libanius the traditional and only true and civilized way of life, which was threatened by an abominable cult. To meet this threat the most effective thing that Libanius could think of was to appeal to the loyalty of the people to their city. In classical times this had been one of the strongest appeals that could be made to a person of Greek culture. The city in Libanius' day could claim this loyalty because Antioch, as he tried to show, was essentially something quite independent of Christianity and of the domination of the imperial administration. Here is an instructive aspect of the working of the classical heritage in antiquity. Julian,

Themistius, and Libanius each had different opportunities. Each followed a different program. We can admire their efforts if we also know, as they did not, that the force against which they were fighting was too strong for them.

If the Hellenistic sculptor Eutychides' bronze figure of the Tyche, the goddess of Good Fortune of Antioch, disappeared—it would be interesting to know how and when it was destroyed—and if the site became a heap of ruins, picked over by Moslem peasants in the middle ages as a quarry for building stones, the city did not wholly perish. Its culture was absorbed in the new Greek Christian civilization. Each of the great cities of the eastern Roman Empire—Antioch, Alexandria, Constantinople—made its own contribution to this new culture; and two of the small university towns, Athens and Gaza, played an essential part. In the end, the contribution of each of these centers was summed up in Constantinople, so Christian an imperial city, and thus was transmitted in due time to the West. But the gift of Constantinople to civilization might not have been quite the same if the other cities had not provided their shares.

What was it, in a word, that made Antioch what it was? Libanius and John Chrysostom both devoted themselves to the study of man and society, but they saw man's social activity in different perspectives and assigned different reasons to it. For Libanius, human society was formed about culture; for Chrysostom, human society was formed about religion. If these two elements could be brought together, as they were in the Antioch of Theodosius the Great, the result would be a city which would possess (in the phrase of J. H. Newman) "the grace stored in Jerusalem and the gifts which radiate from Athens."

SELECTED BIBLIOGRAPHY

Contemporary Sources in Translation:

St. John Chrysostom. Six volumes of selected works in translation are printed in the *Select Library of the Nicene and Post-Nicene Fathers of the Christian Church*, First Series, Buffalo, 1886–1900, reprinted recently at Grand Rapids by Eerdmans. There is a complete translation of his works in French by the Abbé J. Bareille, *Oeuvres complètes de S. Jean Chrysostome*, 21 vols., Paris, 1864–1878. The treatise *On the Priesthood* is translated by A. J. Moxon, London, published by the Society for Promoting Christian Knowledge for the Fellowship of Saints Alban and Sergius (S.P.C.K.), 1907, and reprinted. The treatise on the education of children is translated by M. L. W. Laistner in his book, *Christianity and Pagan Culture in the Later Roman Empire*, Cornell University Press, 1951. The liturgy attributed to Chrysostom, but probably not entirely written by him, which is still used by the Orthodox church today, is available in a convenient translation, with rubrics, glossary, and introduction, *The Orthodox Liturgy, Being the Divine Liturgy of S. John Chrysostom and S. Basil the Great*. London, S.P.C.K., 1939, and reprinted in 1954.

Libanius. For his encomium of Antioch, quoted above in the text, see "Libanius' Oration in Praise of Antioch (*Oration XI*)," translated with introduction and commentary by G. Downey, *Proceedings of the American Philosophical Society,*

Vol. CIII, No. 5 (October, 1959), 652–86. This contains a bibliography of other translations of works of Libanius into modern languages now available. The important speech *Concerning the Prisoners* is translated by R. A. Pack in his dissertation, *Studies in Libanius and Antiochene Society under Theodosius*, University of Michigan, 1935. A translation and literary study of the *Autobiography* by Mr. Michael Crosby is in preparation.

Theodosius. *The Theodosian Code and Novels*, translated by Clyde Pharr and others. Princeton University Press, 1952.

MODERN STUDIES:

Dohrn, T. *Die Tyche von Antiochia*. Berlin, 1960. An iconographical study of the original statue, and of its influence on classical art.

Downey, G. *Ancient Antioch*. Princeton University Press, 1962.
———. *Constantinople in the Age of Justinian*. University of Oklahoma Press, 1960 (Centers of Civilization Series).
———. *A History of Antioch in Syria from Seleucus to the Arab Conquest*. Princeton University Press, 1961.

Festugière, A. J. *Antioche païenne et chrétienne: Libanius, Chrysostome et les moines de Syrie*. Paris, 1959. An interesting study, containing translations of numerous passages in Libanius, Chrysostom, and other authors. The point of view is highly individual.

Haddad, G. *Aspects of Social Life in Antioch in the Hellenistic-Roman Period*. Dissertation, University of Chicago; New York, Stechert, 1949.

Jaeger, Werner. *Early Christianity and Greek Paideia*. Harvard University Press, 1961. On the absorption of the Hellenic tradition into Christianity, and the formation of a Hellenic-Christian culture.

Jones, A. H. M. *The Greek City from Alexander to Justinian*. Oxford University Press, 1940. On the administration, economic life, and municipal operations of the Greek cities of the eastern Mediterranean area.

King, N. Q. *The Emperor Theodosius and the Establishment of Christianity*. London, S. C. M. Press, 1961.

Levi, Doro. *Antioch Mosaic Pavements*. 2 vols. Princeton University Press, 1947. The complete corpus of the mosaics.

Mumford, Louis. *The City in History: Its Origins, Its Transformations, and Its Prospects*. New York, Harcourt, Brace and World, 1961. An original and perceptive study of the city from earliest times to the present.

Petit, P. *Les étudiants de Libanius: Un professeur de faculté et ses élèves au Bas Empire*. Paris, 1956.

———. *Libanius et la vie municipale à Antioche au IVe siècle après J.-C.* Paris, 1955.

Piganiol, A. *L'Empire chrétien, 325–395*. Paris, 1947. The best general history of the fourth century.

Walden, J. W. H. *The Universities of Ancient Greece*. New York, Scribner, 1909. The best study in English of education in Libanius' time and of Libanius' own education and teaching career.

Wolff, H. J. *Roman Law: An Historical Introduction*. University of Oklahoma Press, 1951.

INDEX

Aetolia, colonists from: 13

Alexander the Great: 8, 12, 92; coins, 116

Alexandria: 3, 6, 22, 57, 156

Ammianus Marcellinus: 3, 78

Anthusa, mother of John Chrysostom: 107

Antiochus I, king: 30

Antiochus III, king: 6

Antiochus IV, king: 6, 31

Apamea: 10

Arcadius, prince: 125

Aristophanes: 50, 90

Aristotle: 7, 60, 152

Arius, heresiarch: 111f.

Athanasius, St.: 49

Athens: 3, 6, 12, 28, 57, 64f., 83f., 92, 104, 151, 156

Augustus, emperor: 13, 17

Aurelian, emperor: 38, 41

Babylas, St., bishop: 32, 103; martyrium, 35; church, 103

Barnabas, at Antioch: 15

Basil, St., of Caesarea: 54, 86, 89, 112, 114, 132, 154

Beroea: 5, 17

Berytus, law school: 66

Celsus, governor: 124

Christians, name of: 14

Chrysostom: *see* John Chrysostom

Cicero: 51

Clement of Alexandria: 53

Clement, St., of Rome: 53

Commodus, emperor: 22; bath, 24

Constantine the Great, emperor: 25, 38, 41, 43, 45, 48, 56, 86, 110f., 144f., 149; church, 25, 27, 103, 119, 121, 135

Constantinople: 3, 6, 27, 57f., 64, 68, 79, 150f., 156; palace, 26; foundation, 41; university, 59; law school, 66; Council of, 381, 112

Constantius, emperor: 25f., 48, 80, 89f.

Corinth: 50

Cossutius, Roman engineer: 30

Crete, colonists from: 13

Cyril, bishop: 144

Daphne, maiden: 34
Daphne, suburb: 6, 9f., 16, 29–33;
   Jewish community, 13
Decius, emperor: 32
Diocletian, emperior: 26f., 38,
   41–43, 86, 144f.; palaces, 26f.,
   35
Diodorus of Tarsus: 108

Eleazer, Jewish priest: 30
Elis: 92
Euboea, colonists from: 13
Euphorion of Chalcis: 6
Eusebius of Caesarea: 45, 86
Eutychides of Sicyon: 28, 84, 156

Flavian, St., bishop: 110, 124, 126,
   128f.
Fortune of Antioch: *see* Tyche
   of Antioch

Gaius, jurist: 66
Galerius, caesar: 145
Gallus, caesar: 32
Gaza: 4, 156
Gibbon, Edward: 101
Gorgonius, count: 26
Gregorian Code: 66
Gregory, St., of Nazianzus: 54,
   89, 112, 114
Gregory, St., of Nyssa: 54, 112,
   114

Hadrian, emperor: 35
Herakleis, old name of Daphne:
   33
Hermogenian Code: 66

Herod, king: 17
Homer: 63

Ignatius, St., bishop: 32
Isocrates: 93f.

Jerusalem: 15, 156, destruction,
   31, 35; Temple, 31
Jewish community: 13–15, 30,
   117, 122f.
John Chrysostom: 85f., 103–32,
   137–39, 146f., 149f., 152–54,
   156
Jovian, emperor: 80
Julian, emperor: 25, 32, 34, 49,
   59, 75, 80, 86–89, 95, 97, 115,
   147, 154f.
Julius Caesar: 22; basilica, 22, 24
Justin Martyr, St.: 53
Justinian the Great, emperor: 56,
   149f.

Laodicea-on-the-Sea: 10, 127
Libanius: 6, 14, 16, 19, 21, 26,
   36, 50f., 58, 66, 72, 77, 79, 82
   84, 85–102, 104, 130, 132, 144,
   146f., 149–51, 153f., 156
Lysippus: 28

Maccabees, martyrs: 30, 123
Macedonia, colonists from: 12
Meletius, St., bishop: 32, 107,
   109f.
Miletus, *bouleuterion*: 29
Modeim, Palestine: 31

Nemesius of Emesa: 131f.
Newman, J. H.: 156

Nicaea, Council of 325: 47, 90, 111
Nicomedia, Libanius at: 90
Nikolaos of Damascus: 6

Origen: 53

Palladius, biographer of John Chrysostom: 109
Palmyra, colonnaded street: 17
Papinian, jurist: 66
Paul, St., at Antioch: 15, 28
Paulus, jurist: 66
Pausanias of Damascus: 6
Peter, St., at Antioch: 15
Plato: 82, 152
Pliny the Younger: 14
Plutarchus, governor: 25
Pontius Pilate: 153
Posidonius of Apamea: 6
Protagorides of Cyzicus: 6

Romanus, St., martyr: 145
Rome: 58

Seleucia Pieria: 5, 10f.
Seleucus I, king: 4, 9–12, 16f., 27f., 30, 34, 92

Spalato, palace of Diocletian: 26
Strabo: 6
Symeon Stylites, St., church: 26
Synesius of Cyrene: 86
Syrus, hermit: 109

Tertullian: 53
Themistius: 49, 59, 82, 86–89, 91, 95, 97f., 153f., 156
Theodosian Code: 66
Theodosius the Great, emperor: 32, 39, 49, 56, 66, 80f., 99, 110, 112, 123, 125, 128, 146–50, 156
Theophilus, governor: 124
Thessalonica, palace: 26
Tiberius, emperor: 17, 21
Titus, emperor: 31, 35
Trajan, emperor: 22, 30, 32, 95
Tyche, of Antioch: 28, 30, 83f., 156

Ulpian, jurist: 66

Valens, emperor: 22, 24, 49, 80–82, 94, 123
Valentinian, emperor: 24, 80
Vespasian, emperor: 24, 35